MUSIC IN EDUCATION

THE WOBURN EDUCATION SERIES

General Editor:
Peter Gordon, Institute of Education, University of London

Games and Simulations in Action
Alec Davison & Peter Gordon

The Education of Gifted Children
David Hopkinson

Slow Learners: A Break in the Circle
A Practical Guide for Teachers in Secondary Schools
Diane Griffin

The Middle School: High Road or Dead End?
John Burrows

Teaching and Learning Mathematics
Peter G. Dean

Music in Education
A Guide for Parents and Teachers
Malcolm Carlton

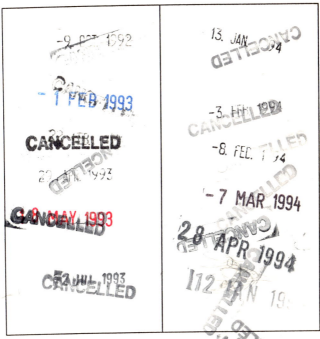

MUSIC IN EDUCATION

A Guide for Parents and Teachers

MALCOLM CARLTON

THE WOBURN PRESS

First published 1987 in Great Britain by
THE WOBURN PRESS
Gainsborough House, Gainsborough Road,
London E11 1RS, England

and in the United States of America by
THE WOBURN PRESS
c/o Biblio Distribution Centre
81 Adams Drive, P.O. Box 327, Totowa, N.J. 07511

British Library Cataloguing in Publication Data

Carlton, Malcolm
    Music in education: a guide for parents
    and teachers.—(The Woburn education
    series)
    1. Music—Instruction and study
    I. Title
    780'.71   MT1

    ISBN 0-7130-0155-0
    ISBN 0-7130-4009-2 Pbk

0049477

374.78
CAR

136132   Printed in Great Britain by
          A. Wheaton & Co. Ltd., Exeter

'Music takes over where words leave off'
Mendelssohn

Contents

Acknowledgments

I should like to acknowledge my debt of gratitude to Dr Peter Gordon without whose guidance this book would not have been written. I should also like to thank Victor Payne for the many constructive suggestions which have been incorporated into the final version. My thanks are also due to my former colleagues, to those who at various stages have typed the manuscript and to all my past pupils and students who have provided the experience on which this book is based.

Finally I would like to thank Dorothy for being a constant source of encouragement and inspiration.

M.C.

Thanks are due to the following for permission to use extracts from copyright material: to Universal Edition (London) Ltd. for extracts from *New Sounds in Class* by George Self; to Universal Edition (Canada) Ltd. for extracts from *Ear Cleaning* and *Rhinoceros in the Classroom* both by R. M. Schafer; to Heinemann Educational Books for extracts from *The Intelligence of Feeling* by Robert W. Witkin; to Bell and Hyman for extracts from *Sense and Sensitivity* by Alice Yardley and *Music and the Young School Leaver*, Schools Council Working Paper 35; and to Macmillan and the Schools Council School Curriculum Development Committee for extracts from *Gifted Children in the Primary School* by the Schools Council.

Foreword

This book is for parents, teachers and others involved in the education of children. It aims to provide, in easily understood language, a guide to music in education; it includes some historical detail, but is mostly concerned with what actually occurs or ought to occur in the classroom in both primary and secondary schools.

Parents will find it a useful aid in establishing what they might reasonably expect for their children, whereas teachers may refer to it for help in designing a curriculum or organizing activities. For others involved in education it will provide a broad view of an often misunderstood area of education, and hopefully remove some layers of mystique which have become encrusted over the years.

The English education system is still in a transition period where the age of transfer from primary to secondary school varies according to geographical area, but for the purpose of this book the traditional transfer age of 11 years has been adopted.

As the reader will see from the Contents page, the book is organized in the following way. The first section encompasses pre-school and primary education. Specific examples of curriculum for 5/6 and 9/10 year olds, together with suggested resource material, are given in Chapter 2, while Chapter 3 considers in more depth the elements of singing, listening, creating, and how they might be implemented.

Chapters 6 to 12 cover the various aspects of secondary education and range from a brief study of some influences on curriculum development from the 1960s onwards to curriculum planning, content, implementation and assessment; the contribution made by so-called 'extra-curricular' activities is considered in Chapter 11. The most important changes resulting from new thinking, the influence of pop and rock, and advances in technology, are examples of some of the aspects discussed.

Although Chapter 13, 'Musically gifted pupils', is to be found in the Secondary Education section, it will certainly also be of interest to teachers and parents of younger children.

It is appreciated that readers may refer to various chapters which are relevant to their specific interests, and therefore viewpoints have in some cases been duplicated in other sections; for the same reason, lists of references and further reading/resources are included at the end of each chapter.

Introduction

Communication through Sound

Music is a non-verbal language, a way of communicating ideas and feelings through the medium of sound. Babies communicate feelings long before being able to use words; parents quickly learn to identify sounds which indicate hunger, pain, cold, frustration, insecurity or contentment. This is a natural and basic way of expressing feelings, a way positively discouraged by a society which uses words as the main language of communication. Words rarely seem adequate to express extremes of emotion, for example in moments of fear the immediate reaction is to scream to release some of the tension. Other experiences involving a build up of tension cause all but the most inhibited to respond to a release with some vocal utterance, sounds which convey much in personal feelings particularly where another person is closely linked with the experience. Many inhibited people suppress the expression of feelings to such an extent that they possibly never develop fully as individuals; as a direct result many experiences in life are totally inaccessible to them. Part of the role of music in education is to help people to overcome this suppression without suggesting an unleashing of emotions in an uncontrolled way. The need is to help individuals to organize and express feelings and ideas in a manner which is compatible with the society in which they live.

There is a tendency to underestimate the ability to communicate through sound; for many people music can be a most powerful and intense language of communication. In addition to transmitting feelings of extreme emotion, it has the power to uplift whole nations to achieve seemingly impossible feats, for example the music of Sibelius and the Finns; for others it is able to provide an escape from reality.

Music is potentially an area of education which can contribute towards emotional and intellectual development. It has, therefore, the opportunity to make a substantial contribution towards the development of an individual and as a result help the person to live a richer and fuller life. This thinking is not new, but only recently has it begun to affect curriculum development in school. Music teachers have in the past protected music as an isolated and rigidly structured recreative subject without accepting that it is part of a much larger curriculum and total educative process.

PART ONE

PRE-SCHOOL AND PRIMARY
EDUCATION

CHAPTER ONE

The First Five Years

... particularly for parents to read

The pre-school child, at nursery or home, can only benefit from a rich aggregation of music experience. There are some experiences to be shared by parent and child; there are others for children to discover and experience for themselves, but which depend on the appropriate opportunity being provided.

However, without parents providing anything exceptional, most young children are subjected to a number of musical experiences. As a direct result they reach school age with a wider experience of sound than is generally realized, a good deal of it accruing from the mass media. From television children hear a variety of musical styles ranging from electronic sound patterns used as a background for a science fiction series to simple advertising slogans usually referred to as 'jingles'. They will probably have experienced the emotional response which music is capable of stimulating, for example, by creating tension at a critical point in a film.

Many will have shared songs with pop stars simply by 'singing-along' with radio, television, record or cassette. Regrettably, fewer children are arriving at school with a repertoire of nursery rhymes; the influence of the mass media has dictated that few parents now actually sing to and with their children, and although 'singing-along' has replaced this, it could be argued that children are deprived of an extremely sensitive act of communication with their parents.

The majority of children live within urban areas and will have contact with music provided to accompany shoppers in supermarkets and department stores, and travellers in railway stations. In Western civilization there appears to be a need to fill almost every moment with sound, a contrast with many Eastern cultures where quiet meditation plays a major role in the way of life. Many primitive societies have used sound to keep evil away, so perhaps today's society is attempting to do the same by using music to dissipate the pressures of twentieth century living patterns. The tendency is for listening to be entirely unselective, a process to which a large number of young children are subjected.

This then is the range of experience which most children take with them to school, but such wide exposure to sound can and does produce a major identifiable problem. A young child is very aware of sound and is readily attracted by anything new; from the age of a few weeks the head will quickly turn to identify the source of a sound. A constant background of music can however dull this response very early in life and accordingly may tarnish awareness of the environment in general. A dulling of sensitivity in one area may affect sensitivity in other areas; if the blunting occurs at an early age, the emerging adult is likely to be less than a complete person. Awareness of surroundings and of other people would appear to be a fairly basic requirement of life.

In practical terms can anything be done to counteract this process? To restrict or prevent listening would be negative, but a great deal can be done to provide children with the opportunity to experience the raw materials of music individually and practically; in other words music from the media reaches children second-hand and this needs to be supplemented by first-hand experience.

Rattles are one of the first instruments or sound sources with which a child will experiment. The need to shake, throw out of the pram, observe and listen to the impact it makes, are all ways of finding out the limitations of the 'instrument', even where the action of throwing appears to be a direct result of frustration or of devising a game to gain attention.

But is it noise or is it music? The dividing line varies according to individual viewpoints. The raw materials of music are sound and silence; it could be said that music exists when a predetermined length of time is filled with these elements either in a carefully organized or entirely random way, but if so what is noise? Noise to one person may be sweet music to another; the sound of a baby crying at night may disturb a person in a nearby room and cause feelings of frustration and anger, but to the mother, especially if it is a first child, this could be a most welcome and reassuring sound. Murray Schafer, the Canadian music educationist, in his book *Ear Cleaning* (1967), puts forward the view that noise is simply unwanted sound which prevents the individual from hearing what he wants to hear, for example an unsuppressed electrical device interfering with hi-fi listening, a form of aural pollution. A parent able to accept this definition may find it easier to see the relevance of providing and permitting suitable experiences for a young child.

Other 'instruments' are discovered, for example at mealtimes the possibilities of sounds from cup and spoon are exploited instinctively. At some point, almost all children sit on the floor with a collection of saucepans and lids together with other kitchen utensils, and from these materials organize, in a seemingly unbearable way for the parent, a 'piece of music' from the sound. The music may appear to the adult to have no structure and to make no logical sense, but it must be remembered that a child is relatively unconditioned at this age by either formal structure, conventional scales or rhythms. It is first essential for any individual, adult or child, to explore an instrument to establish possibilities in terms of sound potential. Familiarity helps; playing with saucepans once is not enough; only after repeated experience and exploration will there emerge any possibility of organizing the sound to any effective and satisfying degree. To the parent, it may appear to be meaningless play, but to the trained observer considerable development may be seen. It is imperative that parents do not interfere by showing the child how to organize sound in a way which conforms with ideas of the adult mind, although it would be reasonable to help the child discover some of the sound potential.

In the pre-school period, then, the parent ought to surround the child with a variety of sound making materials and allow exploration and experimentation. This contact with the raw materials of music is as basic as allowing a child to explore and discover through sand, water or paint.

A question of some concern for parents is whether very young children should learn to play 'real' instruments. It is thought by some that in order to produce top class performers, training must begin at an early age, although this is not necessarily the case.

A three year old insisted on having a violin for a birthday present having seen and heard one on a television programme. Although there were no musicians in the family, it became apparent that nothing else would satisfy the child and so the parents duly made a purchase. Child and violin became constant companions, even to the extent of the instrument being taken to bed complete with case. The parents were sensitive enough to search for a teacher who was sympathetic and able to help the child explore the instrument. The teacher in turn made it clear to the parents that if the child displayed any sign of losing interest or enthusiasm, then that would be an appropriate time to consider releasing both pupil and teacher from the commitment. This did in fact occur, but it is worth conjecturing that at some time in the future the child will return to the instrument to build on the early experience.

Woodwind and brass players rarely start before they reach the upper end of the primary school; the reasons for this are largely due to the physical problems created by the size of the instruments, the necessity to guard against teeth realignment, and the possibility of causing physical stress such as lung damage, although this point is often disputed by teachers.

Many parents are aware of their own musical inadequacy. This very fact may make it easier for them to see how children's musical skills develop, whereas the highly trained musician, who has undergone a formal musical education, can find it difficult to adjust to these levels. The qualities required of a parent are those of patience, awareness and a constant willingness to encourage.

To summarize, activities provided for the child should include a substantial amount of singing experience, preferably some together with the parent, an opportunity to explore a wide range of sound making materials, and focussing attention on the natural sounds of the environment in which he lives. The pneumatic drill is part of the city child's environment and therefore not necessarily a sound from which to withdraw; on the other hand, a town dweller would benefit from a visit to a contrasting environment. Faced with unfamiliar surroundings, a first reaction is to be more aware visually than aurally, and unless assisted by the parent or teacher, the child may not be fully conscious of the sounds created by, for example, a gently flowing stream or by shoes treading on bracken.

Pre-school children should be encouraged to take advantage of modern technology and use battery operated cassette recorders with built-in microphones to record and play back sounds both of their own making and those already made. The development of pocket size synthesizers of the *Casio* type is an exciting one, for they are both safe and stimulating to use.

The constant addition of experiences can lead to a growing facility to select from those which please, stimulate and excite, an essential part of the process of expressing ideas and feelings through music.

How the experience gained can be developed will be seen in the following two chapters, but it can be said that this growth of experience is reflected in an ability to absorb all that is around, much of which a less aware person may live through without recognizing its existence. The true value of this enrichment can only be appreciated by those who possess it.

REFERENCES

Schafer, R. Murray, *Ear Cleaning*, Universal Edition (Canada) Ltd., 1967.

SUGGESTED FURTHER READING

Ash, B., Winn, A. and Hutchinson, K., *Discovering with Young Children*, Elek, 1971.
Chazan, M., *Education in the Early Years*, University College of Swansea, 1973.
Crowe, B., *The Playgroup Movement*, George Allen & Unwin, 1973.
Kent, J. and P., *Nursery Schools for All*, Ward Lock Educational, 1970.
Parry, M. and Archer, H., *Pre-School Education*, Schools Council Research Studies, Macmillan, 1974.
Phillips, J., *Give Your Child Music*, Elek, 1979.

CHAPTER TWO

Music in the Primary Schools (5–11 years)

... mostly for teachers but containing useful information for parents

In 1969 a group of primary teachers made this statement:

Education must not be a substitute for living but living itself. We must ensure that it includes spiritual, emotional, intellectual and physical development, in fact, the whole child. There must be opportunity for growth in every aspect of the person ... Education is not only the acquiring of skills, but also the development of feeling and sensitivity, which requires flexibility in the individual ... Whatever way we choose to organize, there must be freedom for individual development, flexibility so that no child feels he is being forced into a pattern that is unacceptable to him as a person. Too often in the past children have become distressed because of their inability to conform. (*The Worcestershire First Schools*)

It does not require much imagination to see how music can contribute to the development of the qualities listed, but then the same claim might be made of other subject areas; so it could be argued that unless a subject offers a unique contribution, it is merely duplicating other areas of learning and experience.

Music is a means of communication and therefore a form of language which communicates directly through its own language rather than by words, and it is particularly concerned with emotions and feelings. The uniqueness of this language reinforces the view that it should be part of the curriculum for every child. Further to this, as will be shown later in Chapter 9, p.95, music education is able to contribute towards developing qualities ultimately sought by potential employers, but which also are beneficial to any emerging adult. This process begins during the early years of education and not much later as is often assumed by both parents and teachers.

Alice Yardley has this to say in her book *Sense and Sensitivity* (1970):

the education of feeling doesn't just happen, it needs as much attention as any other form of development. If we hope for the child above all to have an adequate intellectual adjustment to his world, then we must educate him to feel as well as think. We can merely pass through experiences, or we can be fully aware of them ... However many people who are influential in educational affairs do not recognise the importance of feeling. In some, deep personal feeling has never really awakened and they plan for children along the lines of their own limited education.

This inability to feel deeply or become fully involved emotionally with experiences and indeed with other people may in part stem from a negative attitude adopted by school towards aesthetic areas of work. Few people can live without music apart from those deprived by the disability of deafness, but regrettably for many it has to be a listening and reacting role, rather than one of any practical significance. Children and adults are able to feel intensely about music which they have created individually or in a group. Deep emotional experience may be gained from involvement in a practical way, experience which can start on the initiative of the child at an early age (see Chapter 1, p. 5), and which needs to be nurtured and encouraged to grow rather than be stifled by the teacher; when encouraged and not driven, the child will react and respond to surroundings in her* own way. The satisfaction gained from this experience together with the feelings generated can only increase awareness and sensitivity to the environment and community surrounding the child (see Chapter 1, p. 6). Many individuals live mundane lives and are unable to react to their environment; if education is a preparation for life ahead, then music has a real part to play in the development of awareness and feeling. Individuals grow to be the people they are as a result of the experiences they live through; pure knowledge itself is insufficient. Some of the most intense and deeply felt experiences can arise from a curriculum which allows the creative arts, and music in particular, to flourish and be on a par with other subject areas.

Attitudes still exist which reflect the view that music's place is outside the curriculum and its function is to provide recreation and relaxation after the essential work has been completed. There are basically two reasons why music may be considered to be a

*The feminine and masculine pronouns are used alternately to refer to both male and female pupils and teachers.

dispensable luxury. The first is undoubtedly lack of thought and understanding by some teachers of this age range concerning the part music has to play in the overall development of the child; secondly, there is a strong feeling by many teachers that they would be unable to cope with the work involved. A mystique surrounds music in education, a mystique built over the years by music teachers, which perpetuates the view that it is largely concerned with teaching actual techniques, for example, how to play the recorder, and that such teaching demands highly trained specialists. However, this is not so. There is a place for the specialist in a primary school, but a substantial part of music activity will continue to be stimulated and activated by the class teacher. Specialist musicians follow a rigorous and relatively rigid training which, if transferred to the primary school, could have disastrous results; conversely the fresh musically untrained mind of the non-specialist may be able to associate more readily through music with the developing child. Personal skills such as the ability to play the piano, recorder or guitar are welcome but inessential for the primary class teacher. As with parents, the qualities required of these teachers are exactly those it is hoped to develop in children – awareness, flexibility and imagination.

The role of the teacher is to be a catalyst for musical activities rather than a person who instils facts and musical techniques. It is evident that teachers shy away from musical activity and yet, objectively reviewing their own education, many are critical of a curriculum which starved them of this experience. A lack of confidence on the part of the teacher may show itself in a reluctance to interfere with work in progress, and this in turn may be the very way which will assist a child to choose an individual path.

ORGANIZATIONAL DIFFICULTIES

Few if any organizational problems arise with more formal activities which involve the whole class such as singing, but at any age the prospect of permitting thirty or more children, all in one room, to individually express ideas in sound is a daunting one. This can and does take place successfully in many secondary schools, but in the primary school, where open-ended timetables exist, several areas of learning may be taking place at any one time, and then viable alternatives may have to be sought.

Very young children who are new to school obviously cannot be allowed to work in areas away from immediate contact with the teacher and so in this case activity must take place in the teaching room. Noise levels of work at this age tend to be greater than at later stages and children move freely from one activity to another, so practical work is less likely to disturb others. It is important to have a range of instruments available for children to use, but it is pointless to fill the music corner with instruments which encourage loud penetrating sounds to be made to the discomfort of others, for example a snare drum and wooden sticks or a pair of cymbals to clash together; an alternative would be to provide a wire brush or soft beaters for the snare drum and to place a single cymbal on a stand to be used with the same beaters. Drums with hard sticks could be introduced at a formal, large group session.

For older children, would it not be better for a smaller group of say six children to work at any one time or should individual activity in music occur for the whole class at the same time? Another possibility might be to allow pupils to work individually as and when the need arises. Whatever the solution, sound levels are the nub of the problem; sound from one area may totally destroy other creative or formal work in process. The dulling of senses has already been commented on in Chapter 1, p. 4, and although children are able to concentrate on work at home despite constant background music from radio and television, school may be unconsciously contributing to the desensitizing of pupils by suggesting on the one hand that they have the opportunity to explore and become more aware, yet at the same time expecting others to switch off from the sounds surrounding them.

The provision of a separate area is a great help, but in many buildings space is at a premium. Some schools make full use of corridors and cloakrooms for music work where they are in the vicinity of the classroom. In one particular school, staff and pupils have accepted that the corridor will be a constant hubbub of musical activity and it appears to have little if any disturbing effect on children working in the classrooms.

Another large primary school operating in open plan buildings has organized specific half days each week for creative activities across the age ranges, a development which allows children to work in family/ vertical groups. Children select from the various alternatives and merge with other groups where appropriate.

These are examples of possible solutions, but it is essential for each school to examine its particular circumstances before deciding how each class is to implement this area of activity. The problems identified can be overcome in almost all situations if the determination to do so is there and if conviction about the value and importance of the work is upheld. It is worth noting that creativity is not so much spontaneous reaction as something which emerges from systematic and regular involvement.

MUSIC CURRICULUM

The language of music is that of sound and the curriculum ought to be designed to provide children with the widest possible experience of working in that medium. The various components of the music curriculum, for example, performing, listening and composing, should link together naturally as they arise from the general aims of the scheme of work; concepts such as colour, dynamics and rhythm recur in the varied activities and are continually reviewed, reinforced and extended. Teachers frequently find it difficult not only to design a curriculum for music education but also to know how best to present such a document. An example of aims and objectives together with content for two classes, namely 5/6 and 9/10 year olds, follows. It must be stressed that this is only a suggested method of presentation, but one which could be adapted to the requirements of any school.

A MUSIC CURRICULUM FOR A PRIMARY SCHOOL

Aim

Through the language of music to contribute to the overall development of each child within the aims for education as defined by the school.

Objectives (how the aim is achieved)

To provide children with the widest possible experience of the language of music and sound, and thereby develop:

a. aural perception;
b. the ability both to receive and to communicate through the language;
c. imagination, awareness and feeling;

d. practical skills;

e. social skills through group work;

f. the ability to be selective and make decisions.

Notes

Wide experience will be gained as a result of:

1. listening in all its aspects ranging from recorded music to live music created by pupils;
2. performance including singing and playing;
3. composing/creating starting with exploratory work and leading to organized composition.

a. *Aural perception* is the ability to listen perceptively; all music in education is concerned with the development of this ability. The ear is fundamental to receiving sounds, communicating through sound and discriminating in performance or in composition.

b. *Communication* will largely arise from composition; the ability to communicate personal ideas and feelings to others may also develop through performance.

c. *Imagination, awareness and feeling* are qualities which will develop directly as a result of compositional work but are also closely related to listening experiences.

d. *Practical skills* will emerge as a result of performance and from composition activities.

e. The majority of subject areas within the school curriculum aim towards children working independently of each other, whereas in the 'real' world of the adult, most people's work patterns are essentially collaborative. The need to work together and make *joint decisions* is a quality sought by employers; group activity particularly in composition is able to contribute towards this.

Content (how objectives will be achieved)

General Notes

1. Where possible music activities should arise naturally from other curriculum work in progress or the reverse may occur. However these links should be natural and never forced; unrelated music activity is equally justifiable.
2. To make an impact on individual development, music activity should in the early years have a daily input, however small, and in

later years it is suggested at least on three occasions a week.
3. It is assumed that each classroom will have a music corner or table containing a variety of sound making materials ranging from tambourines to home made instruments.

Curriculum Content for Reception Class (5/6 year olds)
Activities for the whole class or large groups

Singing

1. Action songs.
2. Nursery rhymes.
3. Singing games.

Accompaniment (if any) by the teacher using any of the following: guitar, piano, recorder, auto-harp, glockenspiel, pocket synthesiser.

Instrument work

These activities would include use of body sounds such as clapping, finger snapping.

1. Games, for example imitation of sounds and rhythms and identifying hidden sounds.
2. Creating effects for use before, during or to conclude songs, for example the sound of a harvesting machine using woodblocks, scrapers and home-made shakers, or snow-falling sounds utilising glockenspiels/chime bars as the sound source.
3. Songs with small groups of children providing simple pulse accompaniments or more complex as appropriate.
4. Playing along with records or tapes. Again these would be mostly pulse patterns, but would provide wide experience of feeling different speeds and types of rhythm, for example reggae, polka, rock and roll.

Listening

1. Short extracts of recorded music to listen and move to, for example electronic sound patterns, space music, African drumming, music from Bali, folk songs and those from the top twenty pop charts.
2. Classroom sounds. Identifying and recording these to develop awareness of surroundings; later applying the same process to sounds around the school in general and the environment beyond.

3. Live music where possible such as by visiting musicians, school music groups both from own and nearby schools and compositions by pupils of all age ranges.

Small group or individual activities

Any of the above mentioned activities could be used and particularly individual listening through headphones. Other activities could include:

1. Exploring qualities of sound capable of being produced by various materials such as chime bars, plastic bottles filled with different grains, for example dried peas or rice.
2. Using an adjacent portable cassette to record, listen and reorganize sounds.
3. Using pocket synthesisers, particularly those with built-in rhythm patterns.

A series of picture work cards would guide and stimulate activity ranging from encouraging children to try out some of the sounds to organizing and selecting sounds which they prefer.

For evaluation and assessment of this work, refer to Chapter 10, p. 99, but achievements should include developing the following short pieces, each being of not more than one minute's duration:

1. Using two different textures, for example, a chime bar and a wood block.
2. Developing ostinati (short repeated rhythmical patterns) and adding a second as an accompaniment.
3. Discriminating between short and long sounds and using the discovery in composition.
4. Making pieces containing regular pulse patterns and linking with a metronome, electronic if possible.
5. Inventing sounds to accompany a story.

Suggested resources for 5/6 year olds

Bley, E. S., *The Best Singing Games* (for children of all ages), Sterling, New York, 1973.

Burlton, L. and Hughes, W., *Music Play* (learning for young children), Addison-Wesley, 1971.

Challis, E., *Jumping, Laughing, Resting* (ages 3–10) (songs for a new generation series), Oak, New York, 1974.

Collini, E. and Corretti, G., *Make Music*, Arnold–Wheaton, 1983.

Gilbert, J., *Musical Starting Points with Young Children*, Ward Lock, 1981.

Glatt, L., *What To Do Until The Music Teacher Comes*, Berandol, Canada, 1978.

Green, A. H., *Guitar in the Primary School* – a course in guitar accompaniment, O.U.P., 1975.

Hope-Brown, M., *Activities in music with children under six*, Evans, 1976.

ILEA, *Sounds Together, Sounds Unlimited*, Inner London Education Authority, Teachers Music Centre, Sutherland St., London SW1.

McMorland, A., *The Funny Family* (songs, rhymes and games for children), Ward Lock, 1978.

Nelson, E. L., *Holiday Singing and Dancing Games*, Sterling, New York, 1980.

Powell, H., *Game-Songs with Prof 'Doggs' Troupe* (*44 songs and games with activities*), A. and C. Black, 1983.

Tillman, J., *Kokoeoko* (songs and activities for young children), Macmillan, 1983.

Curriculum Content for the 5th Year (9/10 year olds)

Singing

A wide repertoire of songs including folk, traditional and pop. Accompaniments by the pupils – relatively complex following four years' growth of experience; both rhythmical and melodic accompaniments organized by the teacher or invented by the pupils. A full range of classroom instruments should be available and the ability of recorder players, string players and others having instrumental lessons must be fully exploited in the classroom.

Instrumental playing

In addition to song accompaniments, classroom pieces will include, for example, chime bar pieces, improvised work, playing of pieces invented by others in class or group work.

Listening

Listening is part of all performance but there will also be listening to a wide range of recorded music, for example film sound tracks, Penderecki and Pink Floyd.

Environmental sound projects, more complex than earlier years with results developing into compositions.

Sound games, for example imitation of rhythms and passing sounds round the group.

Composing

It is again assumed that there has been steady development over the four previous years, otherwise there will be a need to begin at the exploratory stage. Achievements should include:

1. Composing sound to accompany a series of tape slides or video film.
2. Accompaniment to stories or plays.
3. Individual compositions using pocket synthesisers or other available electronic devices or computer.
4. Group composition to support projects in hand.
5. Group composition using, for example, shape, a picture, a rhythmical figure or a cartoon as a stimulus.

For evaluation and assessment of this work refer to Chapter 10, p. 99.

Suggested resources for 9/10 year olds

Allen, W., *Music Games*, Cambridge Educational, 1982.

Barratt, S., and Hodge, S., *The Tinder Box Assembly Book (Starting Points, Stories, Poems and Classroom Activities)*, A. & C. Black, 1982.

Bley, E. S., *The Best Singing Games* (for children of all ages), Sterling, New York, 1973.

Challis, E., *Fun Songs, Rounds and Harmony* (ages 8–14), Oak, New York, 1974.

Dankworth, A., *Voices and Instruments*, Hart-Davis Educational, 1973.

Dobbs, J., Fiske, R., and Lane, M., *Ears and Eyes*, O.U.P., 1974.

Gadsby, D. and Harrop, B., *Flying Around* (88 rounds and partner songs), A. & C. Black, 1982.

Gilbert, J., *Musical Starting Points with Young Children*, Ward Lock, 1981.

Glatt, L., *What To Do Until The Music Teacher Comes*, Berandol, Canada, 1978.

Green, A. H., *Guitar in the Primary School* (a course in guitar accompaniment), O.U.P., 1975.

ILEA, *Choosing and Using Classroom Instruments*, 1980. *Sounds Together. Sounds Unlimited.* Inner London Education Authority, Teachers Music Centre, Sutherland Street, London SW1.

McMorland, A., *The Funny Family* (songs, rhymes and games for children), Ward Lock, 1978.

Mendoza, A., *Hey Betty Martin* (songs for children to sing and play), Curwen, 1977.

Osborne, N., *Creative Projects* (for middle school), Chappell, 1981.

Paynter, E. and J., *The Dance and the Drum* (integrated projects in music, dance and drama for schools), Universal, 1974.

Schools Council, *Time for Music* (a structured music programme arising from the Schools Council project 'Music Education of Young Children'), Edward Arnold, 1977.

Sounds Natural (a world wild life songbook), Boosey & Hawkes, 1983.

Tillman, J., *Exploring Sound*, Stainer & Bell, 1976.

Walker, R., *Sound Projects*, O.U.P., 1976.

Making instruments

Blocksidge, K., *Making Musical Apparatus and Instruments*, British Association for Early Childhood Education, 1957/74.

Dalby, S., *Make Your Own Musical Instruments*, Batsford, 1978.

Dankworth, A., *Voices and Instruments*, Hart-Davis Educational, 1973.

Mandell, M. and Wood, R. F., *Make Your Own Musical Instruments*, Sterling, New York, 1983.

Romney, E., *The Musical Instrument Recipe Book*, Penguin Education, 1974.

LEARNING TO READ MUSIC

Many teachers in primary schools are expected to teach children to read music. Facility to read music may be interpreted as being able to identify the names and values of notes, but it could also be the ability to read music at sight fluently; so it is important to establish precisely what is meant by those exerting pressure.

Children can be quickly taught the names of notes and their values, for example E is the bottom line of the treble clef and the note is a minim and lasts for two beats – there is no mystery about this, but the process beyond is a very complex one and no one has yet devised an effective method of teaching 'reading' whether desirable or not. The actual stages of reading music can be seen as the linking of:

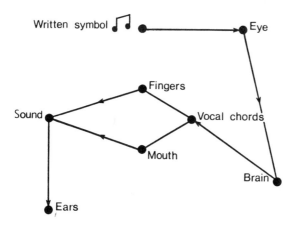

... a far more complicated process than, for example, the reading of words. With the spoken word, pupils in primary schools would expect to have daily practice in order to develop fluency, so it becomes obvious how unrealistic it would be to expect similar achievements in music without at least daily practice.

There is little doubt that 99% of 'readers' develop the ability as a result of and parallel with instrumental playing experience, and usually without undue emphasis being applied to reading.

Notation is an aide-memoire and therefore teachers must be wary of insisting that pupils keep their eyes glued to the music. It is important that music is taught through the ear and not the eye, and where children are able to commit music to memory as soon as possible, then the ear will be able to concentrate on intonation, quality of sound, interpretation and feel.

It would be unusual, to say the least, to see an actor performing with script in hand once a play had opened and it would be fairly unusual to see a concert pianist using a music score. Most rock bands never use written music, and one such band consisting of top flight musicians, who can all read fluently, merely uses a few graphic sketches. In fact after repetition through rehearsals the majority of professional musicians commit whole or part to memory, and from then on do not actually read the music – it is there as a prop.

The value of being able to read music is undisputed, but its position in the curriculum needs to be viewed in perspective. Some further discussion which may be helpful to the reader will be found in Chapter 9, p. 94.

INTEGRATION WITH OTHER SUBJECT AREAS

The word rejection is almost synonymous with adolescence; school music comes high on the rejection list as will be seen in Chapter 8, p. 70, and yet there is a whole teenage subculture centred around the world of pop music. Children in the middle years of the primary school frequently show signs of rejecting music before any other area of work. This may be caused by pupils becoming generally more self-conscious and reacting against activities which require practical participation, but yet the same children play games and compete in athletics. A more likely explanation is that the curriculum may have the wrong emphasis, music being treated as an area of little obvious importance to be introduced only if spare moments can be found, and where the content is clearly separate from other areas of the curriculum. When this occurs it is hardly surprising that, in the eyes of pupils, school music appears to have little purpose; if on the other hand music evolves from and integrates easily with other areas of work, then there is less reason for the separation to take place in the pupil's mind. Such separation is usually introduced by a teacher as a result of the way she interprets the curriculum, and consequently her attitude may be crucial in overcoming this problem.

The examples illustrated below show how music can link with and emerge naturally from school visits or from topic work generally. First, a school visit to a Tudor house, which could lead to a music theatre piece in the form of a pageant, possibly involving the whole school. There follows a project based on a visit to a local factory; industrial archeology lies at the centre, but the visual and aural experience of real machines will provide stimulus for music activity. Third, an exploration of the whole issue of selling through advertising. Both commercial radio and television make extensive use of music as a persuasive factor in the process, and here pupils have an opportunity to create their own 'jingles'. Tales of mystery and

Tudor living — leading to a pageant

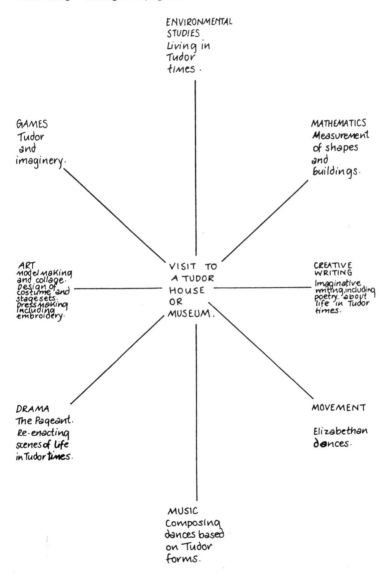

ENVIRONMENTAL
STUDIES
Living in
Tudor
times.

GAMES
Tudor
and
imaginery.

MATHEMATICS
Measurement
of shapes
and
buildings.

ART
model making
and collage.
Design of
costume and
stage sets.
Dress making
Including
embroidery.

VISIT TO
A TUDOR
HOUSE
OR
MUSEUM.

CREATIVE
WRITING
Imaginative
writing, including
poetry, about
life in Tudor
times.

DRAMA
The Pageant.
Re-enacting
scenes of life
in Tudor times.

MOVEMENT

Elizabethan
dances.

MUSIC
Composing
dances based
on Tudor
forms.

Local Industry

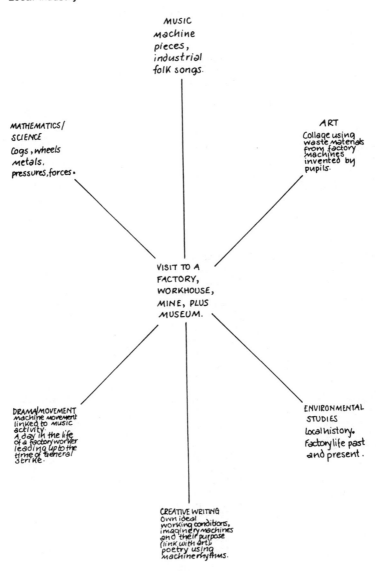

MUSIC
Machine
pieces,
industrial
folk songs.

MATHEMATICS/
SCIENCE
Cogs, wheels
metals,
pressures, forces.

ART
Collage using
waste materials
from factory
machines
invented by
pupils.

VISIT TO A
FACTORY,
WORKHOUSE,
MINE, PLUS
MUSEUM.

DRAMA/MOVEMENT
machine movement
linked to music
activity.
A day in the life
of a factory worker
leading up to the
time of general
strike.

ENVIRONMENTAL
STUDIES
Local history.
Factory life past
and present.

CREATIVE WRITING
Own ideal
working conditions,
imaginery machines
and their purpose
(link with art).
poetry using
machine rhythms.

Television advertising

Aim:- To produce a series of advertisements suitable for use on television.

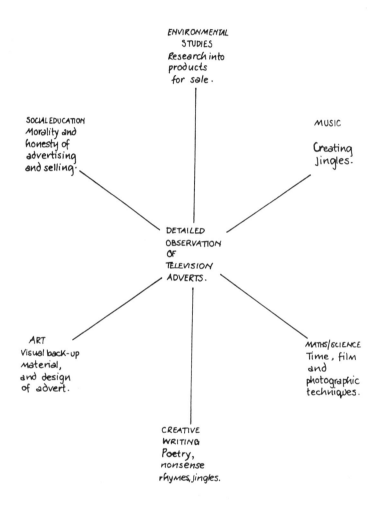

ENVIRONMENTAL
STUDIES
Research into
products
for sale.

SOCIAL EDUCATION
Morality and
honesty of
advertising
and selling.

MUSIC

Creating
Jingles.

DETAILED
OBSERVATION
OF
TELEVISION
ADVERTS.

ART
Visual back-up
material,
and design
of advert.

MATHS/SCIENCE
Time, film
and
photographic
techniques.

CREATIVE
WRITING
Poetry,
nonsense
rhymes, jingles.

Hallowe'en

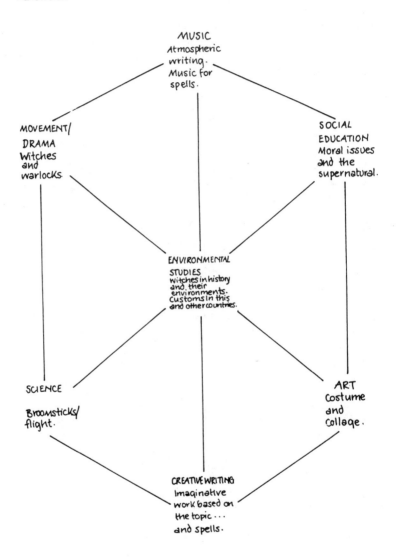

Aim: To explore folklore surrounding Hallowe'en.

imagination hold a fascination for most people and in the final example Hallowe'en is used as a basis for a project which particularly stimulates highly imaginative use of art work, words and music.

Further themes which may be used as a basis for extensive integrated work are Weather, Water, Travel, Circus, Animals, Conservation, Battles, Events in Local History, The Recording Industry, Communication, Natural Phenomena, The Creation.

REFERENCES

Central Advisory Council for Education, *Children in their Primary Schools* (the Plowden Report), HMSO, 1967.
Department of Education and Science, *Primary Education in England*, HMSO, 1978.
'Worcestershire First Schools', unpublished, 1969.
Yardley, A., *Sense and Sensitivity*, Evans, 1970.

SUGGESTED FURTHER READING

Chacksfield, K. M., Binns, P. A., and Robins, W. M., *Music Language with Young Children*, Blackwell, 1975.
Chazan, M. (Ed), *Education in the Early Years*, University College of Swansea, 1973.
Horton, J., *Music – British Primary Schools Today* (an Anglo-American project), Macmillan, 1972.

CHAPTER THREE

Singing, Listening, Creating

... supportive information for the music curriculum (see Chapter 2)

It is necessary here to look at singing, listening and creating as separate entities to consider method and content without in any way detracting from the need to integrate music activity and music with other areas of the curriculum.

SINGING

The activity of singing is one from which many children can gain an enormous amount of pleasure, but not all children find it enjoyable. To many, and this includes pupils in the primary school, the very act of being made to sing as part of a large group can be the starting point for rejection of school music. The growth of instrumental music in the classroom is often thought to be the major factor in bringing about the demise of singing as an activity; but even before widespread instrumental innovations in the 1960s, not all pupils were enamoured of class singing. In the hands of an enthusiastic teacher most children in the primary school find singing an enjoyable activity, but there is a tendency for the older boys in particular to reject it sooner than girls. It is difficult to know from where this attitude stems without looking at individual cases, but there are examples of schools which present music activity as an alternative to sport; in these instances the pressure is on boys in particular to pursue the more 'manly' physical activity. It can be seen that curriculum policy in such schools contributes towards rejection. Many secondary teachers come face to face with the result of such attitudes at the time pupils transfer to their schools, and discover that it can take a long time to change their disposition towards music making and singing in particular. Hopefully more schools will join the enlightened and refrain from placing children in a position where such a choice as the one mentioned has to be made at an early age.

Types of song acceptable to children change with the times, but it is nevertheless important to provide a wide range in a variety of styles. The inexperienced and nervous teacher should choose uncomplicated songs containing short lines and some repetition in the tune, ideally a song with a chorus. A piano accompaniment is not essential; in fact it can be distracting for young voices. It is not easy for a younger child to extract a melody line from a piano accompaniment of chords and many children will soon give up the attempt, particularly if the piano is loud. Children hear music performed by professionals on television, radio and records, and so will quickly sense the uncertainty and inadequacy of a keyboard player. The most natural way of learning songs is by imitating another voice, but if the teacher initially lacks confidence to provide this, then a single line melody instrument such as the recorder could be used, while the guitar is an ideal and unobtrusive instrument for providing chordal accompaniment.

Some thoughts on song teaching

Following any necessary verbal introduction, a teacher should sing the complete song to the pupils to demonstrate the aim of the session, and should wait for problems to arise rather than anticipate them at this stage. The children may then be encouraged to hum the song quietly while the teacher sings it through for a second time, but where there is a chorus the group will quickly contribute with words. Encouragement is crucial and by repetition there should be a gradual increase in contribution from the children until they are able to cope with the verse. It is a shared experience; only when the pupils have gained sufficient confidence in handling the new material will they be able to sing without the teacher. To read or say the words together is obviously beneficial and of course there may be further places in the song where a particular difficulty needs to be extracted and treated separately to iron out a problem. The learning process can be very rapid indeed, especially when it is done by imitation of the whole song; it therefore becomes apparent that it is not necessary to break it down into separate lines for teaching purposes.

In general, songs should be taught in the shortest possible time; children soon become accustomed to a particular pace of learning and there would appear to be little value in lengthening the exercise. If a point is reached where the pupils are no longer responding, or if there is little progress, then it is preferable to move on to other work. There is an assimilation process which is part of music learning and of which little is understood; for example, children may have difficulty with a particular song, which the teacher then decides to leave until a later date. It is a common experience to find that when returning to the work after a break of say two or three days, the difficulties have mysteriously been overcome. This phenomenon is well known to musicians and occurs at all stages of development, but it does not necessarily mean that it will automatically occur. The whole pattern of music learning is generally one of constantly returning to matter and approaching it from different angles, each time seemingly taking one step backwards and then three forward (like learning to read).

There is a place for informal and spontaneous singing; groups of people huddled together in times of crisis or for example at football matches, readily and almost instinctively sing. It is an expression of group feeling, perhaps a release of pent-up emotion but a common language of communication. It would seem therefore that people may sing more readily when standing closely together. A group of children widely spaced around a room may feel insecure and be unable to contribute fully to the activity.

Singing not only involves use of voice, but also the ear; only by listening are individuals able to sing in tune, at the same speed and in time with others. The ear is a flexible and compensatory organ, able to adjust to the overall group performance, but it is worth remembering that when singing it is difficult to hear other voices unless they are in close proximity. At the other extreme, to stand next to a person with a powerful voice can mean total obliteration of all other immediate sound. Experimentation with grouping is worthwhile to see whether it improves the quality of singing; working in a circle in the best camp fire tradition is also worth trying.

Songs may be taught with or without copies for pupils; both methods have much to commend them. The method of learning directly from the teacher is referred to as learning by rote. This method is essential for very young children and for poor readers; it is effective with pupils of all ages, possibly because of early learning experiences from the child's mother and perhaps because it also copies the way in which children absorb vast numbers of songs from the radio. The main advantage is that pupils can concentrate fully on the task in hand without the diversion of hand-held copies. For uncomplicated songs this is the quickest way of teaching new material, but supporters of the alternative method have an equally strong case. It can be argued that it is important for children to see copies of words and music, and that this in itself is part of the process which aids reading development. It can indeed be helpful for pupils to see the shape of a tune and develop some idea of how this shape links with the aural experience; with older children, particularly if more complex songs are used, the aid to memory assists quicker learning. Written words should be dispensed with as soon as possible; teachers sometimes forget how quickly children learn and retain. Some individuals do need to have sight of a copy before being able to commit music to memory and they then recall the visual impression when necessary. For others, the ear is sufficient and they memorize simply by listening. Provision must be made for all types of learner.

Teaching points

a. Interesting material
b. Enthusiasm
c. Encouragement
d. Use voice to teach the song
e. Teach the whole song ... not line by line

LISTENING

All music activity is concerned with listening, whether it be to a person's own composition, performance or to the works of others. One of the aims of music education ought to be to develop the ability to listen because it contributes vitally, not only to music, but to many other aspects of learning and of life. In practice, many teachers narrowly interpret listening as playing records and tapes to children, and it is this particular aspect which is to be considered here.

It is widely accepted that the spoken and written word are the most used means of communication, but there are frequent attempts to inspire spoken and written work from children by bombarding them with so-called aesthetic experiences, for example listening to evocative music or looking at paintings. It should be acknowledged that the latter communicate through their own languages, and any attempt to translate into words emotions and reactions aroused could possibly destroy feeling for the music or painting. Striving to find an adequate form of words can become paramount in the child's mind, particularly if this becomes a regular demand. Yes, many musical pieces tell a story, but the preoccupation with searching for words can detract from the ability to absorb music in its own terms and as a consequence lead to a point where the child makes the experience of listening match words rather than reacting in a personal, individual way to the music. The sensitive teacher will recognize whether it is appropriate to discuss a listening experience with a child; it is more than likely that when the music has been absorbed, this will lead naturally to work in other areas, for example, a child may translate ideas and feelings gained from listening into an original piece of sound building or into a collage or a painting. This is not to say that listening experiences should never be discussed; there may often be a necessity to share ideas, but hopefully the teacher will make no attempt to impose ideas on the children.

How to introduce music for listening is an area in which there is much experience, yet observation shows that the experience is rarely used wisely. Explanation and discussion before listening is largely unproductive, not only for the reasons already given, but because ideas formulated by the teacher implant and impose adult feelings and reactions into the mind of the pupil. For example, the teacher may play a tape of part of Stravinsky's *Petrouchka* and proceed to ask the children what is represented by the music. A guessing game may follow ... the composer intended it to represent a fair, but to some children it could represent a nightmare, a conflict or simply a pleasant collage of sound. Eventually one child may stumble on the idea that it is a fair and be praised by the teacher for arriving at the so-called solution.

Children strive to please and may reorganize feelings and thoughts if they think it will assist the relationship with a teacher. It is not always necessary for children to know what is represented by the music, but more important that they are allowed to have personal feelings arising from the listening experience. It is well known that where highly trained musicians are presented with a new piece of music and are asked to comment verbally, their ideas will differ widely as to representation, and yet so often children are required to reach the same conclusions as others in their peer group.

Listening to music may have the greatest impact following a creative experience, and it may be here that the primary school teacher will need to have contact with a music specialist in order to find relevant material. For example if, after a thunderstorm, a group of children have written poetry and created sound patterns relating to their experience, then it would be appropriate to listen to one of Benjamin Britten's storm pieces such as those from either *Saint Nicolas* or *Noyes Fludde*; this in turn may lead to further productive work. The whole listening experience will have been heightened as a result of the previous creative work in both sound and poetry.

What and how much music should be listened to? Some experiences ought to be evolved directly from listening to sounds of the environment. Additionally many homes provide light and pop music, experience which ought to be reinforced and extended by the school. In education, music is frequently and regrettably thought of in terms of serious or classical (a misnomer) music and the remainder; such divisions are adult concepts imposed on children from an early age and have until recently been almost unchallenged within the curriculum. The primary teacher possessing an open mind has the opportunity to provide wide listening experience which includes serious, light, pop, folk and other categories of music. Although no one would question the value of listening to masterpieces from earlier centuries, teachers ought to widen their own repertoire by exploring more 20th century music; it is the music of the present, music related to the environment in which the children live and music which is likely to be closely related to pieces created by the pupils.

For how long can children listen? Again the teacher will have to discern the optimum length of time. The difficulty occurs when listening is organized with a large group where the capacity for absorption varies for each individual. Providing that facilities are available for small groups or individuals to follow up the work, then this difficulty may be overcome. As a general principle, the younger the child the shorter the listening time, but there are so many exceptions that it is impossible to give firm guidelines.

Teaching points

a. Wide variety of material
b. Don't interfere ... allow children to listen without imposing ideas
c. Whole class listening is not always productive

CREATING/COMPOSING

The word creative is often wrongly used; it could be said that all music activity is creative to a degree whether it be original composition or interpretation of music written by others. In education it is generally understood to refer to original work stemming from the child and which is therefore considered to be creative as opposed to being re-creative. The original work is concerned with manipulating and organizing sounds emerging from materials available.

Children need the opportunity to explore the possibilities of sound producing materials as they would with paint, clay and wood before being able to use them productively. There is a need to experiment and use materials in many different ways before each individual can find an adequate way of expressing ideas through sound. It would be unrealistic to provide a group of children, or indeed an individual, with a number of instruments and expect miraculous instant improvised collages of sound reflecting what the child wants to say. The teacher has to provide the opportunity for a child to discover the potential of each instrument being used; this first stage may appear to be very chaotic, aimless and unproductive to the onlooker, but is a stage which leads to the pupil being able to use the materials in a selective and individual way.

Equipment

It is necessary to establish a sound bank or a resource centre of sound from which all classes in the school can draw freely. Sound areas may be set up for each class and instruments ought to be readily available rather than locked away in cupboards or store rooms. The sound bank should include a wide range of pitched instruments, that is to say those which produce identifiable notes, such as chime bars, glocken-spiels and xylophones. Likewise it should include a variety of un-pitched sounds, for example drums of different sizes, tambours, triangles and many of those originating from Latin American music such as claves, chocolo, guiro plus a collection of suspended cymbals and gongs of all sizes if possible. Children should be encouraged to make simple instruments and there are books available to help with this activity (see the list on p. 18). Visits to the local woodyard and scrap metal dealer will provide sources of cheap material in the way of wood offcuts, dowelling, metal tubing and rods for making instruments.

Portable cassette recorders are essential equipment. They provide an excellent means of recording and retaining pupils' work, and in addition they fulfil a need for both composer and performer, by allowing a pupil to become sufficiently detached from an activity to listen more acutely to what has been produced. During composition this critical listening is an important part of the review and refinement process, whereas following a performance, the participant is able to hear an accurate reproduction of what occurred. At a performance many people absorb only a general impression; the same individuals may then listen with almost complete disbelief to a recording of the same event – faulty intonation, lack of precision may suddenly become apparent. The recording, detached from the performance, ensures that it now becomes a purely aural experience.

Relatively inexpensive tape recorders are available at a much lower cost than the average glockenspiel. Most of the portable machines are easy to operate and use alternative sources of power – mains electricity or battery. The latter is essential because of the necessary mobility in the classroom, and battery usage ensures absolute safety, a particularly important point where pupils are concerned. A recorder with a built-in microphone is an additional asset; the quality of recording is usually adequate unless, for a special purpose, a higher standard is required. Children should be permitted to use the machines; most homes possess similar equipment and it will be only a small step forward to ensure that, in school, children value the equipment and use it correctly. All resources such as these the schools rightly want to preserve, but the investment value is in the use they are put to by the pupils.

Part of the work of the school is to teach children to use equipment in a constructive way without constant supervision; on the other hand teaching care and correct handling does not mean teaching a 'right' way for example to play a musical instrument. There is not just one correct way to play a triangle, a drum or a tambourine, though there is an accepted method used in most orchestral playing. Many 20th century composers require players to produce a greater variety of sounds from percussion instruments, sounds for which technique has to be developed.

Instruments are broken even by professionals, but wilful destruction needs to be carefully monitored and broken instruments should be removed as soon as possible and repaired or even adapted to make a new instrument.

Create but create what?

Everyone can compose albeit in a simple way providing that they do not think of composing in terms of imitating the great composers.

Composing music is simply one way of expressing how people feel and think, a way of communicating with others.

It has already been acknowledged that in order to use materials productively, it is first essential to discover the potential of a sound source. This in effect means that children should not only be given the opportunity to work with a particular instrument or group of instruments over a period of time, but should, through carefully designed assignments, be skilfully encouraged to discover and explore the sound source potential. The extensive vocabulary of sound will lead to attractive and colourful work and facilitate the ability of children to communicate ideas.

Much contemporary music is concerned with colour and texture, while tunes and regular rhythmic patterns have a lesser part to play than in the formally designed music of previous centuries. Children are unlikely to produce music in the style of the past unless steered deliberately in that direction, but are more inclined to produce pieces built on colour and texture. If it is melodic then there is a strong possibility that it will be pop influenced and that the pieces may well feature ostinato figures (regular repeated short rhythmic or melodic patterns).

What will and should children create? It must depend on the individual child. For example, a boy aged seven gained immense satisfaction and pleasure from a piece he composed consisting of twenty-three sounds made on a cymbal, a succession of sounds which he then recorded on cassette. His teacher was able to transfer this to a more complex tape recorder and demonstrate how the boy could explore the use of different speeds on the machine, thereby extending the dimension of sound. Compositions may grow spontaneously, or may stem from work in art and craft, poetry written by children, a school visit, or from a play or theatre piece. They may also be a direct result of a series of work cards prepared by the teacher; for example children may be asked to make a piece of music lasting 35 seconds using three chime bars, and consisting of soft continuous sound, or be given a snow picture accompanied by the following instructions:

Imagine you are standing outside on a cold winter's evening. Snow is falling – gently at first but gradually it becomes heavier. Make a piece based on this idea (3 people – 3 instruments only).

Frequently visual images or words are used to stimulate activity but evocation in this way is not always essential; a composition may be representative simply of personal ideas and feelings. Although the teacher should be wary of continually asking, for example, 'What does it represent?', he should not be afraid to discuss the composition. This is where musical training becomes a handicap because it may prevent the specialist from hearing a piece without being analytical in the formal sense; the temptation to mould is great. A musically untrained teacher may be able to see other qualities more clearly without being concerned in any way with techniques. It is crucial that teachers do not impose ideas and opinions or the work becomes that of the teacher rather than that of a child; if guidance is sought, then that is the time to give it. It is possible to say whether a composition is good, bad or ineffective, but it must be remembered that each individual person views a piece of work in relation to her own experience only. The composer's own judgement may change over a period of time as a result of further experience, hence early work is often rejected in retrospect. A teacher may be able to say whether the work communicates anything to her, but this is a limited factor; if there is to be growth, then children, as with all creators, must continually compose. The role of the teacher can best be viewed as one of providing encouragement and facilities for the work to flourish.

For guidance on evaluation and assessment of this work, the reader should refer to Chapter 10, p. 99.

Teaching points

a. Good resources
b. Allow time for exploratory work
c. Provide stimulus ... work cards, pictures as required
d. Encourage
e. Do not impose adult ideas and concepts
f. Do not apply limited assessment criteria based on own experience only.

Other aspects of music in the primary school, instrumental learning, choral activities and preparing for concerts, are discussed in the next chapter.

ME-D

SUGGESTED FURTHER READING

Arnold, J., *The Organisation of Small-group Work in the Classroom*, Schools Council/
    University of York, 1980.
Evans, K., *Creative Singing*, O.U.P., 1971.
Pape, M., *Growing Up With Music* (a detailed record of music activity with groups of
    children under the age of eight), O.U.P., 1970.
Thompson, B., 'Teaching Infants (Music)', *Teachers World*, 25 June 1976.

CHAPTER FOUR

Instrumental Learning, Choral Activities and Concerts

... for everyone, but essential reading for teachers and headteachers

THE RECORDER FAMILY
(descant, treble, tenor and bass)

Recorder playing from an early age is much in evidence in primary schools for two reasons – first, the instruments, particularly the descant but also the treble, are relatively inexpensive and second because of their size they are fairly easy to play. Pupils at the older end of the school are able to cope also with the larger tenor and bass recorders. Large group teaching however is not recommended; it has proved to be unproductive and certainly unbearable for sensitive ears, but smaller groups have been most successful in providing for individual development and interest. The activity aids music reading development in the way indicated in Chapter 2, p. 18, but only where teachers refrain from writing names of notes under the music; this may seem to be a good idea at the time to assist pupils, but in the long term it merely retards development of reading ability.

STRINGS
(violin, viola and cello)

Should a wide range of instrumental learning be made available to children during primary school years? Most educationists would probably conjecture that although desirable, it is unlikely to be fully implemented within a state-financed programme. Where money is available, authorities tend to allocate funds to the area of instrumental teaching which potentially stands to gain most from the introduction of tuition at an early age, that of strings and in particular the violin.

Instrument size is no problem; ¼, ½ and ¾ size violins are available and children easily adapt to a larger instrument as their body grows. An early beginning would appear to be necessary if only because of the need to co-ordinate ears and hands; the fingers have to find the exact place on the strings for a note, whereas with woodwind, brass and keyboards, keys at least assist to a certain extent. Precision is crucial on the violin for correct intonation; a millimetre either way will produce out of tune notes. It can be seen therefore that it requires a highly developed aural ability to cope with all these requirements. A further hurdle for the string player is that of developing the ability to use a bow correctly with the other hand, an extraordinary and unique form of co-ordination. Little wonder that children may make unpleasant sounds initially when learning, but all the more reason why they must be encouraged to listen acutely from the outset. In helping to correct intonation, the piano is of limited value; keyboard instruments are tuned to a system of equal temperament where, for example A sharp and B flat are the identical sound, but string players will quickly point out that these two notes are quite different on the violin. Smaller sizes of viola and cello are also available and therefore are for the same reasons frequently introduced in the primary school.

PIANO AND WOODWIND
(flute, clarinet and oboe)

There are divided views as to whether children should learn to play other instruments at an early age – the piano is an exception because it involves use of hands only and a child can cope and develop according to physical growth. It is a small step to progress from the descant and treble recorder to either flute or clarinet in the latter years of primary school; children are able to overcome breathing difficulties but teachers should be aware of dental problems which can ensue from prolonged wind playing. Advice should be taken from the instrumental teacher, and the child's dentist should be regularly consulted to ensure that, as a result of long periods of wind playing, the teeth are not realigned in a way which may later require corrective treatment. This danger cannot be over-stressed; many instrumental teachers show a lack of awareness of this problem.

The oboe, because of the intense breathing pressure required, should only be undertaken by older primary children under strict supervision and guidance.

BRASS
(trumpet, cornet, euphonium, tenor horn, trombone and tuba)

Similar fears have been expressed about brass instruments and the possibility of lung damage; nevertheless, many are played by older primary children apparently without any ill effects, although this is difficult to affirm in the absence of empirical research. Trumpets and cornets play higher notes and consequently require more air pressure to produce sounds; they can therefore be quite difficult to play. Conversely those instruments which produce lower sounds such as tubas, trombones, euphoniums may be easier but be too large for the children to handle, especially as no half sizes are available. Many brass teachers recommend the tenor horn, a small tuba-like instrument as ideal for beginners in that it is of medium size, and sounds are easy to produce.

As in all matters concerning music in education, it should be noted that there are conflicting views and various schools of thought concerning brass teaching for young players; therefore information from the Local Authority Adviser should be sought before attempting to introduce a programme of work.

VISITING INSTRUMENTAL TEACHERS

Whatever the pattern of instrumental learning, it is very important and is the responsibility of the school, to ensure that maximum benefit is extracted from visits by instrumental teachers. This can be effected in two ways: by instituting essential lines of communication and by providing follow-up activities.

Many parents have experienced frustration at lack of contact with an instrumental teacher, and apparent failure of communication between the instrumental teacher and other teachers at school. Contact and co-operation are vital, particularly during the early stages of learning an instrument. Parents sometimes experience children arriving at home and needing both help and encouragement; if they are musicians they may be able to assist with musical problems, but if they are not players, then they will be unable to provide any aid or advice concerning actual technique. Certainly during the first few months, many young children seek parental company and support during practice sessions; if neither is aware of the aims of the practice, frustration, disillusionment and a strong desire to discontinue lessons can quickly arise. The first step to correct this must be to ensure that contact between parent and teacher can be direct. Some schools and authorities encourage parents to sit and observe lessons during the early stage of learning, but it requires a firm instrumental teacher and sympathetic headteacher to ensure that the relationship between child and instrumental teacher is protected. The advantage of this system is that the teacher is able to show the parent how to help the child, for example in holding the bow correctly or in organizing practice time. From Japan, the Suzuki method (for violin) ensures that both children and parents learn to play together with what can only be described as phenomenally successful results. The introduction of the method in certain areas of this country has likewise led to encouraging developments.

The school in turn has the responsibility of ensuring that visiting teachers are welcomed and are enabled to meet class teachers. Discussion concerning children who have instrumental lessons can only be of mutual benefit, providing that both view the instrumental work as an integral part of the development of the child and not merely as an additional trimming unrelated to the educational programme.

Poor lines of communication contribute towards children losing interest and discontinuing lessons. Likewise lack of follow-up by the school also makes a substantial contribution to the same problem.

The major task as far as the school is concerned is to provide opportunities for pupils to play together, even as beginners, in instrumental ensembles. Playing in a group should benefit a young player in several ways:

1. It provides an aim and therefore an added incentive to learn.
2. It enables a child to work with players of a better standard and therefore see how her own playing could develop.
3. It develops aural awareness, that is, it encourages players to listen acutely and in turn aids the development of accurate intonation.
4. It immediately widens the player's repertoire.
5. Making music is a sociable activity and this in turn brings together children with similar interests; the pleasure to be gained from playing together in a group cannot be overestimated.

Except in large schools where there are so many instrumentalists that some form of grouping by standard is possible, the difficulty for a music teacher is to find appropriate material for an ensemble containing players of varied ability. There is music available from many publishing houses and instrumental teachers' advice should be sought in its selection. The most effective way of providing repertoire is for the teacher to arrange and compose pieces for each ensemble, but this is time consuming, and also demands considerable skill to arrange parts at a level for each individual; again the assistance of the instrumental teacher should be asked for.

Instrumentalists ought to play together at least twice a week if only for a short time (bearing in mind that it is tiring for a young player to hold an instrument). The group need not necessarily take the same shape for all rehearsals, for example one practice weekly should be for strings alone. At other times all instruments could combine and include recorders, glockenspiels, xylophones, in fact any available instruments.

Bringing all instruments together in one ensemble causes problems in choice of keys to suit the majority. Beginner string players use mostly the keys of D and G in which case clarinet players would, because the instrument is a transposing one, find themselves playing in the impossible keys of E and A. Great skill is required, if these keys are to be used, to avoid the constant occurrence of some sharps – hence the need for like instruments to play together in separate groups at least once a week.

BUYING AN INSTRUMENT

It would be the height of folly for a non-string player to buy a violin without first consulting an expert. The same principle applies to all instruments; the expert again could be the instrumental teacher. As a general maxim, would-be purchasers should always be encouraged to buy the best within their financial means. More expensive instruments produce a superior sound; brass and woodwind instruments are usually more accurately tuned and will have a longer life proportionate to the amount paid. Inferior instruments cause a build-up of frustration in players and can be an additional factor in causing pupils to stop having lessons.

In England, many children are able to borrow instruments from schools, but if there is progress and obvious ability, they should be encouraged to purchase their own. Alternatively, there are schemes operated by retail outlets whereby an instrument may be hired for say a period of a year. At the end of that time, the instrument may be returned to the shop without further charge, or if purchased, the amount of rent paid is deducted from the cost.

Advice on the care and cleanliness of instruments should be sought from the instrumental teacher. On no account should repairs be attempted without consultation, however minor they might seem, but it is useful for schools to keep a supply of strings and rosin, and boxes of reeds for wind instruments.

CHORAL ACTIVITIES

Choral groups exist to provide opportunity for those children who want to sing together with others. In the first instance all children should be encouraged to join such an activity, and experience has shown that from then on the choir is likely to become self-selective as some children develop other interests. The aim should be to provide experience for children who want to be involved regardless of ability; enthusiasm rather than capability is the quality sought and from the former the latter should grow. Rejection at any age is a harsh and scarring experience; rejection from the choral group can provoke a life-long apathy and even fear of music-making; therefore the selection only of good voices ought to be deplored. A child who sings out of tune will not correct the problem by being rejected from an exclusive group, but there is a good chance of counteracting the difficulty by allowing her to work with natural and able singers. Similarly a child who produces a poor tone quality will adapt to match that produced overall by the group. Many musicians have experienced being spurred on to higher goals simply by working alongside more gifted performers.

In schools where classes are grouped according to age, choral and instrumental activities have the advantage of allowing large numbers of children to work together effectively across the age ranges. Most schools accept the choir as an integral part of school life and expect regular rehearsals, but hopefully not always to take place outside the normal timetable, that is during lunch hours or after school.

Rehearsals should be in a room sufficiently large to accommodate comfortably the number of children in a choir, and additionally be acoustically sympathetic, that is, in a room which has the ideal amount of resonance. It is best to avoid over-resonant areas (which produce considerable echo), because such rooms will prevent both child and teacher from hearing accurately what is taking place; as a result poor tone, diction and generally inaccurate singing may develop. Each individual will have an ideal in mind but for rehearsal purposes a room with very little resonance (acoustically dry) is preferable.

As a general guide, when a concert is imminent, it is better to rehearse in the concert room or in an area which is acoustically drier than that in which the performance will take place. It should be remembered that the stress of public performance together with the need to adapt to a new acoustic environment can pose enormous problems; for performance any help given by a more resonant room than that normally used at rehearsal will be advantageous. A further point to remember is that resonant halls can change their acoustic properties dramatically at performance times; the larger the audience, and the greater the extent of curtains and drapes used on stage, the more sound is absorbed.

A concert is the culmination of many hours of activity during which children will have experienced the exploration of new material and a gradual familiarization with the music as progressively more layers are uncovered, all spurred on with the aim of performance in mind. It is a useful whip to drive people along with, providing that the teacher remains aware that every moment of each rehearsal should add to the child's experience. Too often the normally alert and lively music teacher becomes a boring instructor when rehearsing. Many a child's reaction to a piece of music has been dulled by the incessant drive to achieve a perfect performance whatever the cost, a desire to turn children into automatons who will reproduce exactly the wish of the teacher. It requires much experience to be able, after long periods of rehearsals, to present a performance which is both fresh and alive, and which conveys obvious enjoyment and commitment by the performers. To many musicians performance is the ultimate goal, but if the final experience falls short of the educational aims then its purpose must be reassessed.

There are many interpretations of the word 'perfection'. For some, perfection is synonymous with accuracy, but there are so many examples of sterile, accurate performances which compare unfavourably with those containing blemishes yet which live and communicate.

A matter requiring skilful judgement is that of rehearsing for an adequate period of time. Too many rehearsals are counter-productive and are likely to destroy freshness in performance; on the other hand insufficient rehearsals sap confidence and prevent children from being able to add a touch of extra gloss at performance. Many children enjoy performing. They enjoy the feeling of occasion and they enjoy being in the limelight; but not all cherish the memory of such pressures, a fact which must never be lost from sight.

Architects apparently find it difficult to judge degrees of resonance and it is surprising how many school halls are built of hard reflective surfaces which echo. When designing school buildings, architects cater for visual appearance, but rarely can the same be said of design in terms of the aural environment. Current building styles make much use of large areas of glass, uncovered interior brickwork and solid ceilings, all being ideal as sound bouncers. They not only contribute to the problem of the music teacher but add to the general noise level of the school. Can anything be done by a school to counteract such difficulties? Use of sound absorbent materials will help and should be added in stages until an acceptable acoustic is reached, for example by using thicker curtains than those already in use, using pinboard on walls or acoustic tiles on walls or ceilings. In smaller areas which are not so open to public view, wall decoration with cardboard egg boxes can work miracles, subject of course to their first being made fire resistant: if finance is available, carpeting the floor should be considered.

CONCERTS

Public performance has an important role to play in the life of a school; how the children benefit from it is a matter for conjecture. Headteachers generally regard the concert as being a shop window for the school and it is unfortunate that the poor music specialist (if there is one) tends to be judged on this limited facet of work; conversely any activity which improves communication between parent, child and school ought to be encouraged. A strong feeling of community spirit centred on the school, uniting these groups, can emerge after a concert has taken place. The combination of music and many children performing can be an irresistible force, yet the act of performance from the child's point of view must be seen in perspective. A head-teacher who continually gives support and witnesses the process of growth throughout the weeks of rehearsal is invaluable, but one who appears only at the final rehearsal and attempts to add the 'final polish' may unwittingly have a disastrous effect on the performers.

IN GENERAL

There is little doubt that primary educators have been the leaders in curriculum design and teaching methods over the last decades, though not in music. At the same time and especially since the 1950s music has begun to play a much larger part in the lives of all people in the western world, more than at any other time in human history, particularly for children and adolescents.

The now defunct Schools Council, formerly a government and local authority financed body whose responsibility it was to set up research projects with a view to giving priority to curriculum development, established two projects for music, one each for primary and secondary education. The first, *Music for Young Children*, was based at Reading University; in 1970, under the series heading *Time for Music*, it produced a highly structured method with emphasis on the development of musical literacy. The materials consist of carefully graded projects designed particularly for non-specialists; they are attractively presented and, because of the unit structure, are easily evaluated. The method claims to train memory and develop listening, creative and physical skills and painlessly stimulate music reading and writing. It aims, too, to build concepts slowly and methodically with imaginative use of sound.

A comparison with the secondary school project (based at York University and described in Chapter 6, p. 58), which takes a very different view of the role music has to play in the development of all children, will substantiate the view that the link between primary and secondary school, as in many other fields, is almost non-existent and will require in the future much more understanding, co-operation and planning from both sectors.

The new technological age is already with us and will no doubt proceed at an ever-growing pace. The opportunities to be grasped by the arts and music in particular now that most schools are equipped with computers (synthesisers in effect), and with an abundance of small and inexpensive electronic instruments available, are immense. The danger is of course that computers might be used merely to teach music information instead of being seen as new instruments to extend the ever-developing language of sound and its manipulation.

Music in primary school is important. It is vital and it has a unique contribution to make to the development of *all* pupils. It is still a Cinderella – it ought to be a giant.

Note

Readers should refer to the following for further information:

1. Evaluation and assessment (Chapter 10, p. 99).
2. The Orff and Kodaly methods (Chapter 6, pp. 52 and 58).

REFERENCES

Graves, R., 'Repertory: Primary Choral Music', *Music in Education*, January, 1978.
Schools Council, *Music for Young Children: Time for Music*, Edward Arnold, 1970.
Suzuki, *Nurtured by Love*, Exposition, New York, 1969.

CHAPTER FIVE

Choosing a Music Specialist
... for headteachers

Younger children are usually taught entirely by the class teacher, a person trained to teach all subject areas including music. In reality the amount of music introduced is limited and rarely prepares pupils adequately for the work they are likely to encounter during the years of secondary education. A solution to this would be to appoint a specialist music teacher, a person able also to contribute to other areas of the curriculum. The role would be that of a co-ordinator; the music work would continue to be carried out by the class teacher but under the general control and guidance of the specialist who would in addition lead the various instrumental, choral and other corporate activities within the school. The specialist could ensure that the children have a wide music experience, encourage teachers to extend and develop their work in that area, and maintain close contact with the secondary school into which the children will progress.

Headteachers appointing music specialists will rarely be expected to carry such a responsibility without guidance from a music adviser, but nevertheless they will have formulated ideas as to the qualities being sought. In addition to those sought of any intending primary school teacher, others can be identified briefly as the following:

1. A person in sympathy with the aims of the particular primary school.
2. An ability to compose. A person able to write songs, instrumental snippets, music theatre pieces and so on, will prove to be a source of great stimulation to the children and the school environment in general.
3. An able practical musician who may or may not have keyboard facility. The ability to play the piano and link this with other

activities is important, but should not necessarily exclude a candidate who has other strong qualities to offer.

4. The ability to play instruments of the recorder family, and a working knowledge of strings and wind instruments in general.
5. The ability to play song accompaniments on the guitar.

Lucky the school that finds a teacher able to offer these qualities together with enthusiasm, commitment and the ability to communicate.

PART TWO

SECONDARY EDUCATION

CHAPTER SIX

Important Influences since the 1960s

... mainly for teachers

Those teaching in secondary schools in the 1950s and early '60s recall the warning signs indicating that all was not well with classroom music. There was a realization that, compared with developments in other subjects, the music curriculum had been left behind. The general pattern was to follow a stereotyped syllabus gleaned from music education bibles of the time and those of previous decades. For example, the Middlesex Education Committee's *Music in Schools* (1935) was still widely used by schools in the Home Counties. The course designed for third year secondary pupils (13/15 year olds) will give some indication of the overall content.

Aural training:
(a) melodic – learning scales.
(b) rhythm and time – exercises in syncopation and barring exercises.
(c) harmony – revision of intervals and cadences.
(d) exercises for class – sight-singing, transposing melodies as a paperwork exercise, dictation, tonic sol-fa and the naming of notes struck on the piano.
(e) melody making – setting music to words and completing tunes.
(f) musical interpretation and appreciation – the further study of melodies, conducting, score reading, contrapuntal music, the sonata, the symphony and the concerto.

In an introduction to the book, Ernest Read wrote:

Music teaching – like the teaching of other subjects – has undergone great change ... Musicians were some considerable time in realizing that the methods by which they themselves learnt their art were not necessarily the best for use by children ... a musically gifted child of five or seven years is ready to begin the study of an instrument ... not so the average child, for whom far more important preparatory work must be undertaken if he is ever to draw level with the gifted child; lively imagination, creative faculty, all these claim attention, for no musical seed will take root unless the soil is ready to receive it.

The sentiments expressed would be appropriate today, particularly those referring to developing lively imagination and creative faculty, but there seemed little opportunity to aspire to these aims within the syllabus. I personally recall such a tome being thrust into my hand in a secondary school in the early '60s. It recommended a staple diet of songs from the National Song Book, some attempt at sight-singing, the learning of rudiments in an academic and non-practical way plus a substantial injection of musical appreciation. Equipment was limited and consisted of a piano, a record player and a set of song books. Aims and objectives were unrealistic in the time allotted, for example for the development of sight-singing skills. Children read books every day to become literate and yet it was maintained that ten minutes once or twice a week would develop similar ability with music reading.

Many music teachers were there by chance simply because they were already actively working as musicians within the community, perhaps as church organists and choirmasters; there was no require-ment until the mid-1960s to undergo a course of training before teaching music in schools. Although many were good, instinctive teachers, particularly so with choral work, a large number were nevertheless limited by their own musical training which they in turn applied to the school curriculum.

Instrumental teaching was relatively new in many schools although rapid expansion was taking place, undoubtedly as a direct result of generally increasing affluence. Readers should refer to Chapter 12, p. 119 for further information about the development of this service.

ORFF SCHULWERK

During the early 1960s the influence of Carl Orff, of *Carmina Burana* fame, was considerable. Orffwork, as it is often referred to, originated from his teaching and that of Gunhild Keetman during the 1930s at the Gunterschule in Munich, where both physical education and eurhythmics were seen as important in co-ordinating the development of childrens' minds and bodies.

Initially, Orffwork leads children through a range of musical experiences whereby they learn to express themselves freely using both voice and restricted instrumental resources. Speech rhythm provides the starting point; words are linked together to form rhythmical phrases, for example:

Oak Tree, Plane Tree, Sycamore, Birch.

This would be used as follows:

1. Repeat (speak) the whole phrase until a rhythmical feeling develops with an underlying pulse.
2. Stress may be added to words as appropriate together with changes in dynamic level, for example, it may be said in a whisper or with a crescendo.
3. The rhythm could then be clapped at the same time as being chanted. When the two are co-ordinated the spoken word may be omitted leaving the rhythmical clapping to stand alone.
4. The short repeated pattern (called an *ostinato*) may be further exploited by using body sounds such as finger clicking, foot stamping or knee slapping.
5. The patterns may then be transferred to instruments.

Using words as a basis, unlimited rhythmical possibilities may be developed which will then contribute towards a vocabulary from which a pupil is able to select ideas for future use. The use of knee slapping and other body sounds requiring physical movement of the hands contributes to the development of playing techniques for classroom instruments.

Pitch (sounds producing identifiable notes) is also introduced at an early stage. Initially this work is based around the pentatonic or five note scale before progressing to the traditional major and minor scales. The pentatonic scale is that of the five black notes on the piano keyboards; an identical pattern may be produced by starting on any note provided that the same number of tones and semitones is maintained as in the black note pattern.

The pentatonic scale is usually associated with oriental music but other cultures use it, as for example can be seen in Scottish folk songs such as 'Auld Lang Syne', 'Comin' Thro' the Rye', and similarly in spirituals such as 'Swing Low Sweet Chariot'. In Orff's method the notes are introduced in strict rotation starting with the two notes which form the interval of a minor third, and then at the next stage the perfect fourth is added. The first two notes therefore could be E and G followed by A. This particular order was selected because they were

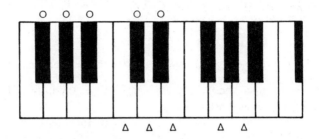

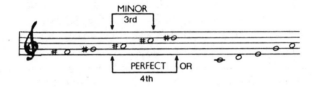

said to be the three notes or intervals used most freely by children during play activities. Exercises are devised in the form of strict imitation of the teacher but lead to question and answer games, the question being posed by the teacher either with voice or instrument and the child replying using available resources, again either voice or instrument; the use of words is optional but may be a useful aid to stimulate activity. When it becomes apparent that the pupils are able to use the permitted notes freely, the range is extended by introducing a new note and the process is then repeated. As a result of constant work with rhythms and patterns, children develop the ability to invent ostinati to which others are able to apply contrasting improvised material.

The Orff movement ensured the introduction on a massive scale of classroom instruments into both primary and secondary schools, instruments which were both sophisticated and superb in quality; this in turn opened up a whole new world of sound potential for every pupil to explore and manipulate. The instruments may be classified into two categories:

Pitched (those able to produce melodic patterns)

1. Wood – xylophones of different ranges, soprano, alto, tenor and bass.
2. Metal – chime bars, glockenspiels and metallophones of similar ranges to the xylophone.

Unpitched

Drums of all shapes and sizes, tambourines, triangles, cymbals, claves, maracas, bells, guiros, woodblocks – the range is almost endless.

Here was an opportunity for pupils to work individually within a group situation and to work creatively; there was scope to express ideas and feelings within a restricted framework. Although geared towards primary children, Orff work was introduced in many secondary schools with great success. For a time the new approach was both stimulating and exciting, but it soon became obvious that the restrictions imposed both melodically and harmonically were too severe. It was also realized that this method was still only a small step forward in terms of curriculum change. Much current thinking decries Orff's work, but viewed from the 1980s it can be seen to have been an important influence in promoting curriculum development.

NEW SOUNDS IN CLASS

A further step forward in the mid-1960s was provided by George Self with the publication of a book of pieces, *New Sounds in Class* (1967), which emerged as a result of his work as a teacher and composer in a North London comprehensive school. Orff's work was acceptable to the majority of teachers if only because it resulted in pleasant sounds being created; use of the pentatonic scale ensured that discords were impossible to produce. It was Self's teaching which unleashed a torrent of activity stimulated by 20th century music. The philosophy behind the pieces in *New Sounds in Class* is outlined in the introductory chapter:

Pupils so often leave school with little knowledge of even the existence of the serious music of their own time and yet for the first time in this century it is possible to introduce avant-garde idioms into the classroom without watering down the style to such an extent that no living music remains.

It is a sad reflection that although many children use their creative energies in painting and poetry, their musical activities are usually confined to performance and listening; with simplified notation it is possible for average children to compose music – and almost this alone should warrant its introduction.

20th century music is concerned primarily with colour and texture as opposed to, for example, music of the 18th and 19th centuries which was based on regular rhythm and on melody related to the major and minor scales. Crotchets, quavers and a five line stave are a convenient way of recording on paper music of these centuries, but are inadequate for notating much 20th century music. It has become essential to develop various forms of graphic notation, forms which most readily and easily communicate the work of the composer. Self used a combination of graphic and conventional notation in his classroom pieces, although it was simplified to enable pupils to interpret scores in a practical way with the minimum amount of rehearsal. He provided an opportunity to express individual ideas freely within a loose framework, ideas unfettered by restrictions of key, of regular rhythm or of crotchets and quavers. The scores were designed to be directed by the pupils and lead to further composition by the participants. Some examples of the notation used are as follows:

●	a short sound or one which dies away almost immediately, for example that of the woodblock.
●⌒	a sound which dies away more slowly, for example a triangle or chime bar.
⋀⋀	a tremolo or sound made by continuously striking the instrument.

Instructions are given in Self's book for producing a variety of sounds – for example, when using small drums, the tremolo effect may be obtained by rubbing the skin lightly with a wire brush or with a wooden stick. The pieces may be played by any available instruments, home made or otherwise, melodic or non-melodic and there are suggested groupings. The scores allow for a wide range of possibilities and require intense concentration and co-ordination on the part of all performers. Individual contribution is limitless within the framework, largely because of the aleatory techniques used. Aleatoric music, a term derived from the Latin root *alea* meaning a dice, is literally music by chance. Improvisation or indeterminacy as it is sometimes called is a technique whereby the composer structures a loose framework which permits the performer to play at least an equal part in creating the composition.

Self's important contribution to curriculum development was continued through a later volume *Make a New Sound* (1976).

OTHER INFLUENCES

In the early 1960s a number of young composers were writing music in an uncompromising style for children. One of the group was Peter Maxwell Davies who was also teaching at Cirencester Grammar School. His work *O Magnum Mysterium* (1961), written for his pupils at Cirencester, was representative of the new attitude towards writing for children. It consisted of four carols and two instrumental sonatas, the latter being composed for both classroom and orchestral instruments; aleatory techniques are used in these sonatas. Those teaching at that time wondered how pupils would cope with the task of performing what appeared to be difficult music written in twentieth century language. In reality, the fresh, untrained mind of the pupil found few barriers to overcome; the problems were only those created by the teachers themselves, undoubtedly because of their own limited music training and experience.

A notable event was the publication in 1970 of *Sound and Silence* by John Paynter and Peter Aston, a book which has proved to be an indispensable reference for many teachers. Subtitled *Classroom Projects in Creative Music* it includes detailed information of thirty-six projects, their preparation, and suggested resource material, and provides examples of work already done by children. Topics covered include music and words, space and time, shapes in music, music by chance, building a chord and night music. Research for this volume originated from the authors' work at York University, a task which was continued by setting up a Schools Council project to promote curriculum development in the secondary school.

An influential figure at this time was the Canadian, Murray Schafer. His approachable books, *Ear Cleaning* (1967), *The Composer in the Classroom* (1965) and later *The Rhinoceros in the Classroom* (1975) stimulated a great deal of thought and discussion about curriculum aims and content (see Chapter 8, p. 72).

In a more traditional vein, the Kodaly method was well publicized and used in a number of schools during this same period. It was concerned with developing aural perception through the use of voice; its success depended largely on regular if not daily practice of the many songs and exercises. The material used is based on the folk traditions of Central Europe and does not always appeal to pupils in English schools.

SCHOOLS COUNCIL PROJECTS

There have been two projects initiated by the Council which have affected music education directly. The first, *Music in the Education of Young Children* (3–11 years), was known as the Reading project because it was based at the university of that name (Chapter 4, p. 45), while the second, *Music in the Secondary School Curriculum*, for pupils of 11–18 years, was likewise referred to as the York project. The aims of the two projects summarize the dichotomy which music teachers have faced during this period. The first was concerned with consolidating ideas on music teaching which have long been practised; it placed emphasis on learning notation and the desirability of children becoming musically literate. Ian Kendall, the deputy director of the project, reporting on progress in the Schools Council *Dialogue* (spring 1976), compared musical literacy to word literacy:

there seems no reason to go on perpetuating the idea that music is too 'hard' for most children to learn. What perhaps has given rise to the idea is the failure of music teachers to break down the learning process into small enough units .... We feel that it is the job of the primary school to tackle this task so that secondary schools can build on the basic skills already acquired.

Aimed at the non-specialist teacher, the project published packs of material containing sufficient material for each class for one year, a tempting and attractive proposition.

The aims of the secondary school project are quite different:

it is concerned with the role that music can play in the total process of secondary education: it is not simply looking for better ways of teaching established techniques. Although music has always been included in the school curriculum, its position has never been carefully defined. It is now recognised that the education of the feelings deserves as much attention as any other aspect of general education. This is an area in which music can play a very significant role. There are considerable sociological implications, not only because of the recreative opportunities that music affords, but also because educators are acutely aware of people's need for self-realization. While recognizing that performance of existing compositions must form an important part of music in school, the project aims also to develop music as a creative activity with pupils exploring the world of sound imaginatively and, by experiment, creating their own structures in sound.

Music in the Secondary School Curriculum, originally to run from 1973–8, was then extended for a further two years. Project planning began early in 1971 and in 1973 local education authorities were invited to nominate schools to participate. Some 200 schools opted to be involved in the development phase of the project. During the first year, representatives of these schools, working with the project team, initiated a pilot scheme for the trial of classroom materials. More schools were later brought in to explore the resource materials. From that time onwards, schools were organized into regional curricular development groups to further effect exchange of ideas and to disseminate philosophy and materials. The extension granted in 1978 was partly to establish a series of ten dissemination centres, the first two being at Homerton College, Cambridge and the City of Birmingham Polytechnic Faculty of Education. The centres were initially contracted to operate for two years but it was the intention of the project team that they should then be adopted by local authorities as regional curriculum development centres, as focal points for teachers and as resource banks.

At the time of writing, the majority of the centres continue to flourish. A number produce twice-yearly magazines which are distributed to all music teachers in the region; they ensure that contact is maintained with the centre and may include classroom pieces, lists of resources available, thoughtful and sometimes provocative comment as well as details of courses available for teachers. With the demise of the Schools Council, the future of some centres must be in doubt, particularly in view of the current economic situation. Those which do survive could well play a crucial role, not only in maintaining curriculum development in the new technological age, but in ensuring that a case continues to be made for music as an essential part of every child's curriculum.

Orff, Self, Murray Schafer and Paynter have been major influences in the changing music curriculum, changes which, as will be seen later (Chapter 8), have been demanded particularly by those on the receiving end, the pupils.

Before considering the formulation of a curriculum, its content and assessment, there follow in the next chapter some thoughts on the shape and size of music rooms as well as comments on instruments which are to be found in the music department. These range from for example, the Orff instruments arising from activities discussed in this chapter to those of the rock band.

REFERENCES

Choksky, I., *The Kodaly Method*, Prentice-Hall, 1974.
Hall, D., *Orff-Schulwerk: Teacher's Manual*, Schott, 1963.
Maxwell Davies, P., *O Magnum Mysterium*, Schott, 1961.
Middlesex Education Committee, *Music in Schools*, O.U.P., 1935.
Paynter, J. and Aston, P., *Sound and Silence*, C.U.P., 1970.
Schafer, R. Murray, *Ear Cleaning*, Universal Edition (Canada) Ltd., 1967.
   The Composer in the Classroom, Universal Edition (Canada) Ltd., 1965.
   The New Soundscape, Universal Edition (Canada) Ltd., 1969.
   The Rhinoceros in the Classroom, Universal Edition (Canada) Ltd., 1975.
   When Words Sing, Universal Edition (Canada) Ltd., 1970.
Self, G., *Make a New Sound*, Universal Edition (London) Ltd., 1976.
   New Sounds in Class, Universal Edition (London) Ltd., 1967.
Vajda, C., *The Kodaly Way to Music*, Boosey and Hawkes, 1974.

CHAPTER SEVEN

Music Rooms and Equipment
... particularly for the financial administrator

English secondary schools vary in size from 400 to 2000-plus pupils and all should have staffing provision for at least one music specialist. The number of music teachers varies according to the size of the school but may also reflect the degree of importance attached to the subject by the headteacher. At its worst the ratio may be as desperate as one specialist to 1000 but at its best it is never likely to be more than one to 400.

Newer schools have facilities for music usually situated away from the main part of the school to avoid the inevitable conflict with other teachers caused by the constant battery of sound. In these schools, music blocks are frequently equipped with adjacent practice or smaller teaching rooms to which groups of children can be dispatched to work on various projects. The Newsom Report, *Half Our Future* (1963) embodied an example of design for a drama, music and art centre which provides a teaching base, practice rooms and a close link with other areas to stimulate the growth of integrated arts work (Fig. 1). The Schools Council Project *Music in the Secondary School Curriculum* included in its dissemination material various tape-slide programmes which were supported by examples of music department design (Figs. 2 and 3).

The majority of schools allocate classes of thirty children to music lessons and although some corporate work is undertaken, the tendency is for work to be structured on an individual or more likely, small group basis. With five or six different activities possibly taking place in one room it might be assumed that this would create an unproductive and unacceptable situation. In reality, pupils do not appear to find it difficult to operate effectively; listening habits which

Figure 1

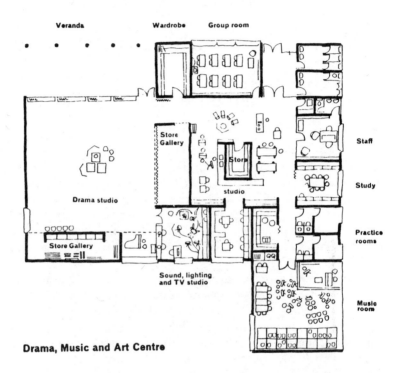

Veranda   Wardrobe   Group room

Store Gallery

Drama studio

Store Gallery

Staff

Study

Practice rooms

Music room

Sound, lighting and TV studio

Drama, Music and Art Centre

enable them to switch off from surrounding distractions become an asset. However one can only conjecture that an environment which provides an opportunity to work away from other projects must surely enable pupils to develop more fully their imaginative and expressive qualities.

There is a need for a teaching room of sufficient size to absorb the array of instruments and equipment in general use. Although sending pupils to other rooms is one way of coping with several small groups, it may mean that it is difficult for the teacher to respond to the groups as and when required. Of course it would be unreasonable to expect pupils to be away from the immediate presence of an inexperienced teacher. It is not essential to provide four sound-proofed walls for each group, but rather an area in which to work, an area which in some way

Figure 2

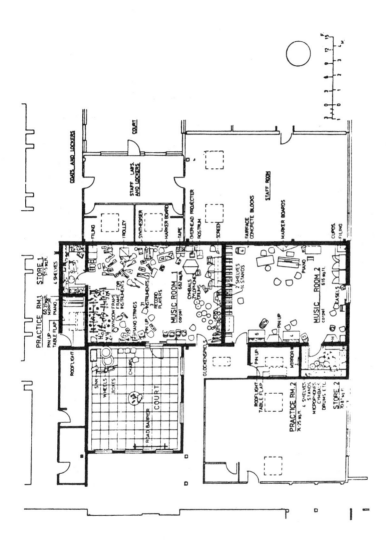

Figure 3

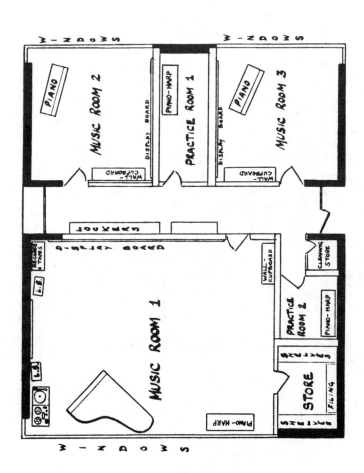

physically separates the groups and which will help to filter out much of the sound produced by others. One solution would be to equip the main teaching room with a series of sound cubicles large enough to take a group of six children, a tape recorder and a supply of instruments. Each cubicle could have an open-door design thereby allowing the teacher to monitor activity, or indeed each cubicle could be linked to a central monitoring point by microphone to enable the teacher to listen in to the work of each group as is the case with language laboratories. It is worth noting that similar screens and cubicles are used in recording studios to prevent the overspill of sound from one microphone to another.

It is however old school buildings which pose the greatest problems; the music room is frequently situated in the middle of the school either next to the administrative offices, the headteacher's room or another subject room. Such a position will probably inhibit the work of the music specialist. In such a case there is little alternative except to ask for a room in a more isolated part of the building, although the introduction of cubicles may go part of the way towards relieving some of the pressure which may occur.

To return to buildings of more recent design, the music specialist could expect to have a major teaching room large enough to enable extra-curricular groups such as choir and orchestra to rehearse without having to transfer instruments and music stands into the school hall. She would also expect to find an acoustically dry room (Chapter 4, p. 42); echo or resonance simply prevents players from hearing accurately. Singers and instrumentalists quickly learn to use acoustics to their advantage and therefore, if performance is the aim, it is crucial to ensure that during the rehearsal stage, little or no help is given by a resonant acoustic. The usual method of correcting over-resonance is to use acoustic tiling on walls or ceiling, but curtains and carpets will also help.

Few secondary schools are without quality record playing equipment. The tape recorder has also become a piece of indispensable hardware particularly where compositional work is taking place. The small portable cassette recorder with a built-in microphone is ideal for instant and unobtrusive recording of material to be played back for critical evaluation. High quality recording is rarely possible on such machines but where the evaluative process is a matter of recording, listening, refining and re-recording, this quality is not essential. The music room of the future may well take on the guise of a virtually permanent recording studio with all compositions being stored by computers and available for instant recall.

KEYBOARD INSTRUMENTS

The diversity of activities and in particular the influence of pop music on the curriculum has compelled schools to extend the range of instruments available to include electric pianos, organs, synthesisers, guitars and necessary supporting equipment such as amplifiers, speaker cabinets, mixing boards, microphones, echo units and other special effects. New instruments, especially those which use the micro-chip, are regularly introduced; it is therefore essential to make regular visits to music shops and to read appropriate journals in order to keep up to date with what is both suitable and available.

During the 1970s and 1980s, the electric piano market was dominated by instruments manufactured under the trade names of Fender Rhodes and Wurlitzer; both possessed distinctive sounds frequently further modified by electronic devices called 'pedals' such as chorus, phase or flange. However the technological revolution has produced digital synthesisers, notably those from Yamaha, which faithfully reproduce the sound of these pianos. The synthesisers are considerably lighter in weight, touch sensitive and are always perfectly in tune; in addition they provide an almost unlimited range of other sounds.

Organs may be a very good second-hand buy if it is evident that an instrument has been used in the home and not been subjected to constant travelling. Preference must be given to an organ which possesses a wide range of tone colour and should include percussion (not to be confused with a rhythm unit). The equivalent to the Fender Rhodes in terms of a classic instrument is the Hammond. In the early models, the sound was produced by tone-wheel generators and consequently they were very heavy and therefore difficult to move. To produce the best sound from an organ it is essential to have a special speaker cabinet called a Leslie (the maker's name) in which the sound is affected either by moving rotors or the speaker horns themselves rotate at a controllable speed.

However, as is the case with electric pianos, synthesisers are capable of reproducing organ sounds. Purists will no doubt hold on to the original instruments for many years, but in general the tendency is to move towards the new technology. The early keyboard synthesiser, which filled a whole room, now has more advanced equivalents which can be carried in one hand. It is likely that these small instruments, some already cheaper than classroom xylophones and glockenspiels, will replace much equipment already used and become, together with the micro-computer, the main sound source for the future.

Where electrical equipment is being used it is the responsibility of the teacher to ensure that all plugs are correctly wired and that all sockets are fitted with saftey cut-out devices; these are not expensive and ought to be compulsory to prevent accidents.

OTHER CLASSROOM INSTRUMENTS

Although the major sound source may change, there will in the foreseeable future be a need for a plentiful supply of both pitched and unpitched percussion instruments. Within the pitched category a mixture of xylophones, glockenspiels and chime bars supported by melodicas and recorders is usual. Bass xylophones are expensive but are a source of good sound potential. Chime bars are best bought individually rather than in sets, because it is then possible to choose the distribution of notes to allow chordal accompaniments to be added to songs. Chords of I, IV and V in the keys of C, F and G should be adequate for most songs.

Key C – Chord I – C, E, G [a]
　　　　　　　IV – F, A, C^1 [b]
　　　　　　　V – G, B, D^1 [c]
Key F – Chord I – F, A, C^1 [b]
　　　　　　　IV – B^b, D, F
　　　　　　　V – C, E, G [a]
Key G – Chord I – G, B, D^1 [c]
　　　　　　　IV – C, E, G [a]
　　　　　　　V – D, F#, A

The letters in brackets indicate how some chords are duplicated; obviously this is a limited choice, but if finance is restricted these fifteen notes provide considerable opportunity for accompaniments in three keys.

Unpitched percussion instruments are required in quantity to provide a wide range of sound sources, for example wood blocks, maracas, claves and tambours. This is an area which can be supplemented successfully by both home made instruments such as shakers made from plastic bottles and by a variety of materials drawn from the environment. A visit to a local scrapyard can be rewarding when building or replenishing resources. Examples of such material are car hubcaps, various lengths of metal bar, sheets of metal, bottles, in fact any material which has sound potential. By collecting resources in this way the financial outlay is minimal.

Apart from the acoustic piano which is provided as a matter of course for every music department, other instruments which tend to be used both in the classroom and for other activities include guitars – acoustic, lead/rhythm electric, and bass – together with a drum kit.

To build up substantial resources demands good long term planning, some vision and wise investment in quality equipment. A well resourced department will be able to support a diverse and imaginatively designed curriculum.

REFERENCES

Bacon, T (ed.), *Rock Hardware Instruments, Equipment and Technology of Rock*, Blandford, 1981.
ILEA, *Choosing and Using Classroom Instruments*, ILEA, 1980 (ILEA, Teachers Music Centre, Sutherland Street, London SW1).

SUGGESTED FURTHER READING

A list of books concerned with the making of musical instruments can be found in Chapter 9.

CHAPTER EIGHT

Towards a Music Curriculum for Adolescents

... some historical background together with aims and objectives

There are no 'official' guidelines for a music curriculum. In many subjects the prospect of public examination at the age of 16 influences, either directly or indirectly, curriculum content throughout secondary education. This need not be so for less than one per cent of 16 year olds sit the public examination in music and only approximately ten per cent learn to play instruments; therefore curriculum design ought to be focussed largely on the remaining ninety per cent.

This relative freedom in curriculum planning is a mixed blessing in that it leaves hard pressed music teachers to survive as best they can, and frequently this means teaching without a relevant, structured curriculum. Many teachers flounder, aware that they ought to keep abreast of current thinking, but too often unable, because of other pressures, to ensure that this occurs. The question of providing a relevant curriculum for adolescents continues to be a matter for vigorous debate; the argument centres on the role music has to play in the overall educative process and how best to design a curriculum which is both acceptable to pupils and which teachers are capable of handling.

Changes, where they have taken place in recent years, show a move away from teacher-directed activities to those which are pupil-centred, with an emphasis on developing imaginative and expressive qualities primarily through composition. A factor militating against this is that of accountability. Traditional teaching programmes are relatively easy to assess, but teachers are only just beginning to get to grips with assessing the more recently introduced activities (Chapter 10, p. 99).

In 1963 the Newsom Report, *Half Our Future*, pinpointed the need to have a long and searching look at the music curriculum:

Out of school, adolescents are enthusiastically engaged in musical self-education ... Yet in schools the contrasts are striking. On the one hand, there are individual schools, or whole areas, where music flourishes, extending beyond the classroom to choirs, orchestras, brass bands, concerts ... pupils and staff, and boys and girls of different ability are brought together in co-operative non-competitive efforts ... by these a sense of unity is fostered, and the individual's range of responses widened. On the other hand, on the evidence of our schools survey, music is the subject most frequently dropped from the curriculum in boys' and mixed school; it is the only subject in the practical group for which one single period is common.

The reasons for this weakness where it exists, appear to be several. One is an unduly narrow conception of the subject ... another is undoubtedly a shortage of suitably qualified music teachers ... Music can clearly be a potent force in the lives of many young people ... and one form of activity which can be carried on from school through adult life; its contribution to both school community and the larger community can be notable. It deserves generous encouragement.

Further impetus was given by a follow-up from the Schools Council *Enquiry I: Young School Leavers* (1968). Written prior to the school leaving age being raised to 16 years of age, it provided evidence of attitudes prevalent both at home and at school. It sought to answer the question posed by Newsom:

Boredom with everything school stands for, or enthusiasm? What is the true picture of the educational situation of hundreds of thousands of young people today?

The report was concerned with pupils of 'average' and 'less than average' ability, that is, those unlikely to stay on at school beyond the minimum leaving age. It demonstrated in no uncertain terms that for a large number of these young people, music was categorized as being the least useful and most uninteresting of all subjects presented in the classroom.

A Schools Council Working Paper written as a direct outcome of Enquiry I, *Music and the Young School Leaver: Problems and Opportunities* (1971), looked closely at the problems of rejection, curriculum in use and new approaches. It accepted the viewpoint that 'usefulness' in the mind of the pupil was a word associated with acquiring skills and knowledge necessary for future employment, a view held less rigidly in schools where the emphasis was placed on 'education for life' as opposed to 'education for living'. This report indicated that if formal education was rejected during adolescence, then no music curriculum could ignore the music that 'young people claim as their own and that they spontaneously and actively enjoy'. The working paper stressed the need to enrich lessons with a variety of experience which would provide a sense of progression and it urged the rejection of music which provoked an unsatisfactory response from pupils. In particular it drew attention to the large amount of 'derivative music (and words) of respectable ancestry but low vitality which no longer appeals either to the discerning music-lover or the uncommitted pupil', a reference in part no doubt to the quantities of poor song material to be found in many cupboards, in some cases a build-up of material from the annual round of competitive music festivals. Secondary teachers were urged to take account of methods being used in primary schools where musical experience arose not only from directed performance but 'from processes of discovery and creation in dealing with sound'. Teachers were reassured that working with instruments was often the quickest and surest way of capturing and retaining the interest of secondary pupils, not only by traditional string and wind, but more particularly through use of Orff type instruments.

The report thought that rejection was part of a large-scale revolt against 'formal school education with its emphasis on the acquisition of intellectual skills and assimilation of inherited culture'. It went on to say that:

Music may be more vulnerable than the other arts because of the prominence of music in the teenager's sub-culture and the conflict between the values of that culture and those of the school.

Nevertheless the report optimistically hoped that for many pupils it was merely a 'detour round the arts'.

Prompted by the Newsom Report, a group of teachers met together in 1966 to set up the North West Regional Development Project, the results of which were later published in *Creative Music Making and the Young School Leaver* (1974). Following an initial survey amongst local teachers, it decided to concentrate research on creative work, although it was accepted that pupils should not learn solely through their own creative experience, but also through the experience of listening and re-creating music. Attempts were made to determine a progression of objectives in both the cognitive (intellectual) and affective (emotional) domains. They were able to clarify the distinction between 'learning' in music and 'learning about', and to make a statement showing how the 'acquisition of knowledge about music' would not aid pupils to a 'greater understanding of music until a later stage' in their development.

Learning in music is a continuous cyclic process, one of constant review and refinement. The need to return time and again to approach quasi-concepts in different ways, whether they be rhythm or form, is acknowledged by many teachers. As far as the creative process is concerned, the report saw the need to try out ideas, to refine them and continue 'exploring, rejecting, reflecting, combining, building'. Amongst other recommendations it urged that music teachers should undergo some composer-training.

In an experimental music course, *Ear Cleaning* (1967), devised by the Canadian composer and teacher Murray Schafer 'to sharpen the ears or to release latent creative energy or both', the view was re-inforced that little is learnt about the 'actual functioning of music by sitting in mute surrender to it'. He writes:

As a practising musician I have come to realise that one learns about sound only by making sound ... The sounds produced may be crude; they may lack form and grace, but they are ours. An actual contact with musical sound is made and this is more vital than the most gluttonous listening programme imaginable ... and the student learns something very practical about the size and shape of things musical.

In a later book, *The Rhinoceros in the Classroom* (1975), Schafer maintains that as every teacher is an individual it is essential to develop a personal philosophy and as a result a curriculum. 'Design one for yourself. A few others may wish to share it with you', he writes. One of the problems facing music teachers is to know what to teach, but Schafer points out that it is only possible to teach things that have already happened; performing music is a reconstruction of the past, a desirable experience, but where does it fit into expressive subjects?

In a knowledge-gaining subject the teacher has all the answers and the student an empty head ... in a class programmed for creation there are no teachers at all; there is only a community of learners. The teacher may initiate a situation by asking a question or setting a problem; after that the role as a teacher is finished. One may continue to participate in the act of discovery but no longer as a teacher, no longer as a person who already knows the answer ... in a class programmed for creativity the teacher must plan for his own extinction.

Music curriculum may in the past have lacked 'balance', and in an effort to rectify this music educators have been compelled to stress the need for creative activity. Inevitably such emphasis has given, quite wrongly in the view of some teachers, the impression that it should form the total programme. Murray Schafer sees two obligations for the music teacher, first to recognize that society will want to keep alive and add to the repertoire of music in existence, and second to tackle an area that music education has failed to acknowledge until recent times.

'Without a Recipe' (1975), an article written by Victor Payne, goes on to develop the point:

The re-creation of music of the past has a valuable part to play ... There is no reason why those who wish to do so should not continue to reproduce it, but the greatest satisfaction of all may well come from taking a few left-over scraps, the bottom of a bottle of wine, a few herbs and proceeding to an end that may just occasionally resemble something that approaches music ... Music is in the process of establishing a new role for itself in an emotionally inhibited and materialistic society that is both alienated against and in desperate need of a greater awareness of man's subjective life ... whatever other claims music may be able to make as an educational force, and there are many, its most valuable function relates to the development of perception and self expression ... It becomes increasingly tempting to serve up prepacked mixtures of instant creativity ... a shallow approach to creative work often provides nothing more than a vehicle for an uncomfortable bout of pentatonic indigestion and helps confuse reality with a directionless flight of fancy.

In an article in *The Guardian* newspaper (1977), Keith Swanwick, Professor of Music in Education at the London University Institute of Education, identified four possible approaches, the first of which he called the 'traditional subject-centred' approach where music is taught through the great musical works of the masters. The second, the child-centred approach, 'often based on foggy ideology', looks towards developing individual qualities which otherwise may remain obscured, while the third, the teacher-centred approach, revolves solely around his own personal enthusiasms. Swanwick maintains that although all have commendable features such exclusiveness 'renders the music teaching far more ineffective than it need be'. He favours the fourth category, the 'situation model':

We have to consider what is relevant and what is appropriate within a situation. What we are trying to do with a certain age-range and in a particular environment.

Robert Witkin, the research director of the Schools Council project *Arts and the Adolescent* from 1969 to 1972, provided some indication in

The Intelligence of Feeling (1974) of the area in which the arts should be making an essential contribution to the curriculum.

There is a world which exists beyond the individual, a world that exists, whether or not he exists, the child needs to know about this world, to move in it and manage himself in it. The curricula of our secondary schools are filled with this world. Everywhere the child turns he encounters the brute facts of history, chemistry, mathematics, and so forth. There is another world, how-ever, a world that exists only because the individual exists. It is the world of his own sensations and feelings. He shares the former world with others ... He shares the second world with no-one ... If his existence in the world disturbs his being in ways that fragment him and render his relationships in the world emotionally confused or even meaningless, then he is ill-adapted, and no amount of intellectual grasp of logical or factual relationships will change that.

So where does this leave the teacher who is attempting to design a curriculum? First it is essential to formulate broad aims from which more specific aims and objectives and finally content may be con-structed. A number of local authorities have produced guidelines for their own teachers, and those for example published by the Inner London Education Authority are well worth consulting. Broad general aims (stage 1) could be as follows:

A   To provide musical activity and experience appropriate to all levels of ability and for the individual development of each pupil in the school community.
B   To provide a range of musical activities which further bond together the school and local community.

These are only examples, but the curriculum designer could then move on in stage 2 to more specific aims/objectives:

A1 To develop aural perception.
A2 To develop practical skills.
A3 To develop expressive qualities.
A4 To develop the ability to work together with others and to develop the ability to make decisions both as an individual and in a group situation (qualities frequently sought by employers).
A5 To develop a curriculum relating to other arts.
A6 To specifically relate the curriculum to the society in which the pupils exist, that is the 20th century.
A7 To encourage a broad and tolerant view of music.
B1 To develop a range of extra-curricular activities open to both

school and local community.

B2 To present a series of public concerts.

B3 To visit local institutions such as old people's homes, feeder schools and shopping centres to present performances.

Before we leave the subject of curriculum aims let it be remembered that for some individuals music is a way of life, a reason for living and a source of inspiration for all that occurs within that person's existence. At different levels of interest, the same may be said of a large number of people, particularly the adolescent who identifies with music for leisure, love, aggression, and as a source of consolation from rejection and being constantly misunderstood by society.

Somehow the music teacher has to arrive at a rationale which envelops this involvement and yet which is both educationally viable and acceptable to the teacher as an individual. The constantly changing attitudes of pupil, teacher, school and society make it essential that this rationale is sufficiently flexible to allow for constant review.

Stage 3 is that of curriculum content, which will be considered in the following chapter.

REFERENCES

Central Advisory Council for Education, *Half Our Future*: the Newsom Report, HMSO, 1963.

Inner London Education Authority, *Music Guidelines*, ILEA, no date.

North West Regional Curriculum Development Project, *Creative Music Making and the Young School Leaver*, Blackie, 1974.

Payne, V. W., 'Without a Recipe', *Music in Education*, Vol. 39, No. 372, March/April 1975.

Ross, M., *Arts and the Adolescent*, Schools Council Working Paper 54, Evans/Methuen, 1975.

Schafer, R. Murray, *Ear Cleaning*, Universal Edition (Canada) Ltd., 1967.
The Rhinoceros in the Classroom, Universal Edition (Canada) Ltd., 1975.

Schools Council, *Enquiry I: Young School Leavers*, HMSO, 1968.

Schools Council, *Music and the Young School Leaver: Problems and Opportunities*, Working Paper 35, Evans/Methuen, 1971.

Soames, N., 'Keith Swanwick talking to Nicolas Soames', *The Guardian*, March 1977.

Witkin, R. W., *The Intelligence of Feeling*, Heinemann Educational, 1974.

SUGGESTED FURTHER READING

Beer, A. S. and Hoffman, M. E., *Teaching Music: What, How, Why*, General Learning Corporation, New York, 1973.

Blacking, J., *How Musical is Man?*, Faber & Faber, 1973.

Brace, G., *Music and the Secondary School Curriculum*, University of Exeter, 1970.

Brocklehurst, B., *Response to Music*, Routledge & Kegan Paul, 1971.

Burnett, M.(Ed.), *Music Education Review*, Vol. 1, Chappell, 1977. Vol. 2, NFER, 1979.

Daunt, S., *Music, School and Young People*, Schools Council Working Paper 3 (concerning the attitudes of young people to the music curriculum), University of York, 1976.

Department of Education and Science, *Music in Schools*, education pamphlet No. 27, HMSO, 1969.

Creative Music in Schools, Reports on Education, No. 63, HMSO, 1970.

Curriculum, 11–16, HMSO, June 1970.

Aspects of Secondary Education, HMSO, 1979.

A view of the Curriculum, HMSO, 1980.

The School Curriculum, HMSO, 1981.

Eisner, E. (Ed.), *The Arts, Human Development and Education*, McCutchan Publishing Corporation, Berkeley, California, 1976.

Gordon, P. (Ed.), *The Study of the Curriculum*, Batsford, 1981.

Gulbenkian, *The Arts in Schools*, Gulbenkian Foundation, 1982.

Jacobs, A., *Music Education Handbook*, Bowker, 1976.

Jones, L., 'Secondary Music Teachers' Attitudes Towards the Teaching of Their Subject', *Journal of Curriculum Studies*, Vol. 7, No. 1, Collins Educational, 1975.

Land, L.R. and Vaughn, M.A., *Music in Today's Classroom: Creating, Listening, Performing*, Harcourt Brace Jovanovich, New York, 1973.

Mursell, J.L., *Human Values in Music Education*, Silver Burdett, New York, 1934.

Paynter, J., *A Place for Music in the Curriculum*, Schools Council, University of York, 1976.

Music in the Secondary School Curriculum, C.U.P., 1982.

Plummeridge, C. (Ed.), *Issues in Music Education*, Bedford Way Papers 3, University of London Institute of Education, 1981.

Schools Council, 'Music and Integrated Studies in the Secondary School', *Occasional Bulletin*, Autumn 1972.

The Common Language of Music (a discussion paper concerned with children's musical development and the influence of their musical environment), University of York, 1976.

The Practical Curriculum, Working Paper 70, Methuen, 1981.

Small, C., *Music–Society–Education*, Calder 1977.

Spencer, P., *The Influence of Creative Music in the Classroom*, Schools Council, University of York, 1974.

Swanwick, K., *A Basis for Musical Education*, NFER, 1979.

Vulliamy, G. and Lee, E., *Pop Music in School*, C.U.P., 1976.

Pop, Rock and Ethnic Music in School, C.U.P., 1982.

Popular Music – A Teacher's Guide, Routledge & Kegan Paul, 1982.

Watson, L., *Supernature*, Coronet/Hodder & Stoughton, 1973.

Whitty, G. and Young, M., *Explorations in the Politics of School Knowledge* (Chapter 2 – What counts as school music?), Nafferton, 1976.

CHAPTER NINE

Curriculum Content in the Secondary School

... performing, composing and listening

For the musician, the task of translating ideas into words is rarely easy but nevertheless has to be undertaken, for example when designing a curriculum. It would of course be unrealistic to set out curriculum content without taking into account the needs of the pupils and the strengths of the teaching staff in a particular school. It is possible to design a curriculum which outlines areas of work or concepts relating to the aims and includes examples of how those areas might be developed without being too specific. The challenge is to design a programme within which both pupils and teachers may work in a flexible way towards the aims already defined. Recent discussion concerning the new 16+ examination which may be introduced in the mid- to late 1980s has prompted many teachers to see curriculum as being divided into three broad sections, each given fairly even weighting for examination purposes; they are *Performance, Listening* and *Composition.* Although these would form a useful basis for constructing a programme, it must be stressed that, for the most part, the three are inseparable activities. Nor must the teacher lose sight of relevance; is the proposed curriculum relevant to the aims and objectives, is it relevant to the pupils, is it relevant in preparing them for life in today's society?

The question of evaluating work will be dealt with later; suffice it to say that the effectiveness of any learning programme must be measured against the original aims and objectives.

A SUGGESTED OUTLINE CURRICULUM
FOR YEARS 1–3 IN THE SECONDARY SCHOOL

Performance

Songs – folk, pop, traditional, in unison, in parts – already published
or arranged by pupil/teacher, adding vocal backing and inter-
jections in pop style and more generally imitating current pop
styles.

Vocal improvisation (composition) – based around chord patterns,
freely improvised to examine particular musical concepts (high/
low or long/short), or to create vocal 'landscapes' or moods.

Vocal pieces and games

Instrumental pieces – percussion pieces, recorder, guitar or rock band
ensembles, combinations of the above but consistently involving instrumentalists with the instrument on which they have
regular lessons.

Instrumental accompaniments – adding accompaniments to songs,
ranging from simple chime bar ostinato figures to complex
instrumental support of other songs.

Instrumental improvisation (composition)

Instrumental games

Multi-media performance – classroom operas; plays with incidental
music; music, film and movement combined.

Performance of compositions.

Composition

The exploration of sound and silence and the various component
parts, rhythm, pitch, amplitude, texture and form using both
vocal and instrumental resources. Starting with short structured
pieces using suggested limited resources, this would lead to
more complex structures with resources being selected by the
composer. A pattern of progression throughout the three years
might reveal the following example:

Year 1 – 30-second pieces using two contrasting textures and
which explore dynamic range.
These would be followed by many other experiences
but may lead to:

Year 2 The addition of a sound track to a 3-minute video film about trains – a wider choice of texture is permitted but the music continues to explore dynamic range and rhythmic concepts.

Year 3 The composition of a 'jingle' which requires concise musical expression (thinking) – a free choice of texture is allowed; again the pupils work with video film, this one being an advertisement for motor cycles.

In these three examples, the progression can be seen in the choice of texture, the widening experience through handling a variety of situations ranging from the initial personal exploration in year 1 to the use of sound as a means not only of communicating personal ideas but as a means of selling a product in year 3.

Other examples might show how electronic music progresses from the use of simple devices such as oscillators and very basic synthesisers to complex synthesised sound, or reveal progression in writing pop songs, composing for the classroom orchestra or for groups of instruments therein.

Listening

This is an essential part of *performance* and of the *composition* process, but additionally listening material is introduced as a stimulus for composition as and when required. An environmental listening project could be used to promote a general awakening of awareness of the environment and consequently be a resource for composition.

Listening to a wide range of music from previous centuries and to that of other cultures is essential but this part of the curriculum will consist of broadening the pupil's experience of 20th century music. The repertoire of this century's music is vast and the programme should include pop, rock music of many styles, mood music, light music, film and television music, opera, musicals (Hollywood and more recent rock), serial music, electronic music and a range of other 'serious' music styles. For example, the curriculum should ensure that pupils are acquainted with the music of Stravinsky, Bartok, Stockhausen, Bessie Smith, Duke Ellington, Jimi Hendrix, Stephen Sondheim and so on.

It does not require much imagination to see how work in all three areas could be devised to be progressive, and how the three are inextricably linked. Some teachers may prefer to underpin the curriculum with a series of concepts possibly to assist with evaluating the programme. They could include:

Rhythm – Regular, irregular, ostinato, polyrhythm, change of speed (accelerando, rallentando), rhythmic patterns (calypso, reggae and in general rock drum patterns).

Pitch – High, low, glissando, ostinato melodic patterns, scales, modes and pitch patterns from other cultures.

Amplitude – Loud, soft, crescendo, diminuendo.

Texture – Sound, silence, single strand to complex, contrasts, vocal, instrumental, electronic, environmental.

Form – Songs, grounds, pieces using visual shapes as graphic representation of sound, binary, ternary, rondo, as required for pupils' compositions. Musical styles generally.

Extra-Curricular Activities

These would depend, not necessarily in order of priority, on the strengths of the teaching staff, a requirement to involve instrumental players in corporate activities and the existing traditions within both school and local community. They may include choir (non-selective), madrigal group (selective), orchestra, wind band.

★   ★   ★

The actual content and experiences provided are important in themselves but are a means to an end, a way of achieving the aims designated; so it is necessary to return to the original aims and objectives to assess whether it is possible to accomplish them by teaching the planned curriculum. If so, each teacher would then need to develop further detailed planning for the next term/half term ahead without losing sight of the aims and objectives.

There now follows further discussion of curriculum content and implementation which includes 'reading music' and 'qualities sought by employers'.

THE CURRICULUM IN DETAIL

Vocal and Instrumental Activities

For many years, singing was the only form of practical music-making which took place in the classroom. The mere act of sitting next to and singing with a person possessing a good voice, can provide a pleasurable experience. On the other hand it can be an experience which many children do not enjoy and they therefore resist involvement. The reasons for this may be many and range from a general lack of singing experience to the personality of the teacher leading the session, but there is no way in which pupils can be made to enjoy singing if they refuse to become fully involved; that is not to say that any attempt would be pointless and in such a situation the teacher must go on trying. Certainly within the last two decades, singing as a class activity has been rejected more than any other practical work by the pupils.

Finding song material which appeals is a difficult task; tastes change and what is acceptable to one generation may not be so to the next. It has already been stated (Chapter 6, p. 52) that the *National Song Book* was for many the staple diet until the mid-1960s. The range of folk songs from the British Isles it contained together with other material from the 16th to 18th century was often supplemented by further volumes of folk song material such as those collected by Cecil Sharp and Ralph Vaughan Williams. Much of the material was very attractive but unsuitable for use in schools largely because of the rural origins of the texts and modal harmonic structure, a far cry from the everyday experiences of the urban schoolchild and the growing influence of popular music. Songs of the great masters, usually in the form of books of 'classical songs' were also used as were the timeless *Oxford Song Book* now republished as *Eyes and Ears*.

Probably the greatest influence in reviving flagging interest in singing activities in the secondary classroom was a series edited by Geoffrey Brace, *Something to Sing*. The first two books, which appeared in the 1960s, were the ones most widely used; their horizons were broader than those of many earlier publications. Folk songs were introduced from a range of countries and most of the material appealed to secondary pupils. The songs were of traditional and more recent folk origin and there were a number of American songs with underlying strong rhythmic patterns. There were songs with which the children could readily identify, such as 'Football Crazy', and others related to television programmes, for example 'Casey Jones'. Suggestions for instrumental accompaniments, or the addition of a second vocal part, were added to each song.

Although one can only generalize, it would appear that singing is again becoming more popular. There are a number of good song books available which contain a fair proportion of usable material but which teachers supplement with other songs usually of the pop variety. 'Head' arrangements – a term used by musicians to describe spontaneous, un-written musical arrangements – can easily be made by adding simple voice parts and rhythmical accompaniments. Songs by the Beatles and Simon and Garfunkel, for example, have become almost part of standard repertoire, but inevitably songs which reach the top twenty come and go fairly quickly, and there would be little point in putting them into song book format for they are likely to be forgotten long before they appear in print. The music teacher has to be an opportunist and grasp attractive songs which will appeal to the pupils but which are also a practical propositon; so many are unusable because they cover an extremely wide vocal range. This approach ensures that pupils and teacher frequently work with new material rather than, as so often in the past, continually revive a limited number of songs. Buskers' books are an invaluable source of varied song material from the 1900s to the 1980s, examples of which are the *101 Hits for Buskers* series and the numerous *Play it again and again and again* books.

Recently a class of 14 year old girls were lethargically attempting to come to terms with an extremely attractive English folk song in a 5/4 metre. Progress was slow and interest waned rapidly. The teacher abandoned the song during the lesson and turned to more popular material, this time a song from the top twenty which was originally taken from a film seen by most of the pupils. The transformation was remarkable; it appeared that all knew the record intimately, and not only were they able to sing the song immediately, but they were also able to cope with rhythmic and melodic inflections, note bending, as well as being able to reproduce the choreography used in the film. The enthusiasm was boundless and one can only conjecture whether this would have carried over to the folk song if there had been sufficient time to return to it. The question of relevance is again apparent; at the time the impact of the song was considerable, but to use it at a later date, perhaps even a matter of months ahead, could produce exactly the same response as that gained by the folk song. From the experience described above, it can be seen that the power of the media and its effect on young people must not be underestimated.

Many teachers look for songs which lend themselves readily to the addition of accompaniments using classroom instruments, accompaniments which are either previously thought out and notated in some form or alternatively are developed by the pupils. These may be simple rhythmic patterns or take the form of harmonic support, for example where chime bars are grouped together to form chords; the repertoire contains a large number of songs based around three chords.

Some songs suggest atmospheric introduction, for example, 'Land of the Silver Birch' from the *Pentatonic Song Book* (1968), edited by Brian Brocklehurst. This would suggest the free use of instruments to form an introduction and possibly a conclusion, while the song itself could have a rhythmic and repetitive accompaniment. Although suggestions are not provided with the songs, here is an example of how the accompaniment might be developed.

Introduction

An element of mystery and wonder is evident in the song – a suitable atmosphere might be created by using suspended cymbals and a variety of beaters and linking the sound with some delicate texture made by either maracas or similar home made instruments. As the introduction builds in volume, a chant, based on the last part of the song, is introduced at first as if in the distance but gradually approaching.

The Song

The introductory texture leads directly into the song during which the accompaniment consists largely of ostinato rhythms taken from the chant or other parts of the song ($\textbf{d}$ $\textbf{d d | d d d}$) or ($\textbf{d d d d}$), and continues as a link between verses.

Conclusion

This would be a reversal of the introduction.

The whole could last somewhere between five and ten minutes and contain a gradual build-up of both tension and volume leading ultimately to gradual release as the conclusion slowly dies away.

By publishing inexpensive pamphlets to link with its radio programmes such as *Time and Tune*, the British Broadcasting Corporation played a significant part in encouraging teachers to add instrumental accompaniments to songs. It went further however by commissioning composers to write what can only be described as mini-classroom operas which contained a good story line, involved singing and playing, gave opportunity for improvisation and could be performed in costume. Two fine examples of these are Carey Blyton's *Konrad of the Mountains* and more notably Gordon Crosse's *Ahmet the Woodseller*. Although this material was intended for primary children, many secondary schools found it to be equally effective for use with their younger pupils. Consequently there is now a considerable range of such material available, a selective list of which may be found at the end of this chapter.

Some further detail of the two mentioned, together with a third, *Drake's Voyage*, by Geoffrey Winters, may provide more insight into what is offered.

Ahmet the Woodseller, commissioned in 1965, is a Moslem story which is 'pervaded with a gentle fatalism'. It tells how Ahmet, a wretched and unhappy man, resolves to kill himself but each attempt is met by failure. Eventually he meets and marries a beautiful princess; the angel of death appears but Ahmet, now a happy and contented person, no longer wishes to die. He successfully cheats the angel by keeping out of the mosque until one day he is summoned to take the place of the Imam who has recently died and so entering the mosque 'Allah receives him into paradise'.

The whole may be performed as a puppet play or alternatively children may act the role of the puppets. The six songs include percussion accompaniments, and classroom instruments are used to illustrate phrases from the dialogue, for example 'he shuddered'. Music is also included for dance.

Konrad of the Mountains, written in 1969, relates how Konrad felled the brutal king of Istria and how each year the village celebrates the anniversary. Again it is a combination of music and dialogue; the instrumental overture represents an alpine band. There are seven songs, including one in three parts; chime bar chordal accompaniments feature in a number of the songs and as with *Ahmet* there is music for a dance. Pupils are required to create an accompaniment for a vaudeville and for the mayor's poem.

Drake's Voyage (1970) concerns the journey which began in 1577 to 'Alexandria to trade in spice', but the 160 men on board were unaware of the Captain's real intentions. There are a number of songs which provide scope for adding further voice parts and the opportunity is given for pupils to create, for example, foggy music or calm sounds. Both conventional and graphic notation are used. A well illustrated map allows pupils to trace the voyage round the Straits of Magellan to San Francisco and back around the Cape of Good Hope.

Since the 1960s, attempts have been made to combine pop styles with the classroom opera format. One of the first and most successful was Herbert Chappell's *Daniel Jazz* (1963), based on the story of Daniel in the lion's den. Since then there have been many imitators but few have been able to produce works of convincing originality. Andrew Lloyd Webber's *Joseph and the Amazing Technicolour Dreamcoat* (1967) has enjoyed enormous commercial success since its original conception; both *Captain Noah and his Floating Zoo* (1970) by Flanders and Horovitz and *Jonah Man Jazz* (1967) by Michael Hurd receive frequent classroom and concert performances.

Still linking words and music but in a different vein, *The Dance and the Drum* by Elizabeth and John Paynter (1974) contains a series of stories, mostly mythological, which aim to provide a basis for music theatre but all the music is created by the pupils. A number of introductory tasks are suggested before an attempt is made at the piece itself, for example, before *The First Sunrise* pupils are encouraged to devote time to discovering 'dark' sounds which describe a 'barren, empty and desolate' world. They are asked to develop 'sun music' and use 'bright sounds' and to listen to the opening of Roberto Gerhard's 3rd symphony as part of the eight suggested preliminary tasks before actually commencing on the project itself.

Many teachers now create their own theatre pieces and make full use of the technology available. Some make their own video programmes, while for live performance others may include projection of photographic slides to link with music and movement.

In the Schools Council Working Paper 35, *Music and the Young School Leaver* (1971), it was stated that:

Many young teachers have built up their own musicianship on instrumental rather than vocal experience, and lack conviction in their attempts to make classes sing with any sense of growing mastery, especially when faced with the problems of adolescent voice ... any corporate musical activity ... demands a concentrated effort of response on the part of everyone engaged in it. The members of an orchestra, a brass band, a choral society ... or a pop group are united in a common task which for the time being absorbs all their energy and concentration. It is far more artificial and difficult to bring about the same degree of unanimity in a mixed ability school class.

Integrating music activity with the other arts as indicated above appeals to young people, and curriculum design in the future, particularly for the older group within a school, may well move more positively in this direction.

Composition

It is difficult for the musician to define clearly the meaning of the word 'creativity'; all music-making must be creative to some degree. Performance of music already written demands creativity on the part of the performer to bring it alive. However, in education the word is used to embrace a much narrower field of activity where children are involved in creating their own music or, in other words, composing. As can be seen from Chapter 6, p. 52, this type of work has only been introduced into the curriculum within the last twenty years or so, and although many established and enlightened teachers regard it as a vital part of their curriculum, the surge of interest is not universal. The very nature of composition demands that pupils are allowed sufficient freedom to develop their own ideas whether individually or in groups. Such a pattern of working requires flexibility in the teacher, particularly if composition has never been part of her own education. For some it may be necessary to establish a situation which initially allows little room for manoeuvre on the part of the pupils, while others may find this unnecessary.

Discipline is often foremost in the mind of a young teacher; the situation is not helped by possible misunderstanding by more senior members of staff of what is happening in the classroom and their tendency to judge a teacher's performance by the amount of noise emerging. A session where pupils are working in small groups may sound chaotic from outside and quite unbearable, but inside thirty children may be completely immersed in the problems they are tackling. The trained observer will quickly recognize whether the overall sound is worknoise or not, but the inexperienced may well find it a difficult task to distinguish the former from the latter.

Discipline is one problem in the mind of the teacher; conviction is certainly another. The usual question which confronts those in education is – I've done that with the children but how do I follow it up, or where does composition lead to? Teachers who ask this question might well ask the same of any aspect of music teaching. The answer is an easy one – all activities, and that includes composition, are means by which the aims of the curriculum are achieved.

If it is accepted that practical experience of sound is fundamental to the curriculum then it can be seen that to restrict activity to performance and listening is to impose severe limitations on pupils' development; it may be compared with providing works of art to look at, a paint brush and an easel but no paint. Music education must also be concerned with the individual playing with, manipulating and organizing sound, that is, being creative and developing further imaginative and expressive qualities through the process of composition.

Working from the sound source is an effective way of introducing compositional work and for this pupils must be given plenty of opportunity to explore available resources. This exploration is a crucial part of the activity; until the full potential of the sound source has been discovered, the scope of creativity is limited. However some pupils will very quickly be able to develop compositions emerging from an idea whereby they seek appropriate sounds to express this, sounds which hopefully are 'imagined' first. Many pupils ultimately settle for a combination of the two methods.

If this type of activity has not been experienced by children during primary education it is more than likely that they will need to be led through the early stages. A series of carefully planned tasks or exercises will usually suffice; for example if a pupil is working with a tambourine, a simple task of discovering ten different sounds or ways of producing sound from the instrument would immediately provide an extended vocabulary to be exploited. The next stage could be to lead the pupils to organising the sounds they have discovered into some sort of shape; for example to take three ways of playing the instrument which most appeal to the player and organize them into a one-minute piece. First attempts may well be crude but as always review and refinement provide a way forward. Almost all composers' first attempts are relatively crude viewed in perspective of later works. Examples of progression in composition may be found in Chapter 9, p. 78; for further illustration of introductory tasks and exercises before projects are undertaken, reference should be made to Chapter 9, p. 85, describing *The Dance and the Drum* by Elizabeth and John Paynter.

Listening

There is a growing concern that the continual output of music in everyday life, such as taped music in the supermarket, railway station or from the radio, may be having a desensitizing effect on young people in particular. Many seem unable to exist without a constant background of music, and many teachers fear that this may contribute to a diminishing awareness of sound. An essential part of the learning process is the ability to listen critically and to react accordingly; even with conversation people frequently listen at a very superficial level or only listen to what they want to hear. It is unlikely that young people who develop these habits at an early age will realize their full potential. One of the aims of music teaching, therefore, is to develop a greater awareness not only of music but also of the environment, and thereby make a significant contribution towards correcting the position already described. Not enough is known about this problem and the two examples which follow demonstrate that learning can take place without a degree of apparent awareness thought necessary.

Recently a class of 13 year olds were asked to identify short taped extracts of sound. They achieved limited success with the exception of one extract which was recognised by all, that of taped music from a supermarket. The particularly interesting point about this was that although the immediate vicinity was served by a number of supermarkets each using background music, the majority of pupils were able to name the actual shop. Without apparently listening or being made to listen, they had identified a particular sound and style merely by being present in the supermarket perhaps only once a week.

The second example is more familiar to parents with adolescent children. Many young people do not appear to listen to the constant background from the radio and yet are familiar with a vast amount of music. For example, as a result many know the tune and words of the ever changing top twenty pop songs, and are able to identify styles of various bands and groups. This simply points to the fact that there are more ways of listening, absorbing and understanding than is generally realized, ways which are only now becoming evident as a result of the phenomenal growth of the music industry.

We are encircled by sound; from a seemingly inseparable collage the human ear has the ability to select and focus. In a room filled with conversation, the ear can focus easily on a discourse it wants to hear and will relegate other conversation to a more distant level. It has the ability to listen to one conversation intently, to another at a lower level of volume and to ignore completely other sounds in the same room even to the extent of totally shutting off. The ear can pick up sounds coming from any direction, although if by some illusion the source is hidden, then a form of emotional disturbance takes place until the direction at least is located. The ability to be selective can be illustrated by comparing two individuals placed in the same room, one possessing normal hearing, the other a deaf person using a hearing aid. The deaf person has no choice but to hear levels of conversation exactly as they occur from the point at which he is positioned; he has no ability to be selective. Beyond this, a person with normal hearing will find it fairly easy to watch a television programme and have some conversation with others in the same room (because of the ability to focus), whereas the deaf person will find this difficult and frequently impossible. To survive in this age, this ability to be selective is essential, but it becomes all the more important to ensure that during early life, it is not subjected to abuse.

Appreciation

The musical appreciation movement brought to this country from America by Stewart Macpherson at the turn of the century continues to influence the curriculum in many schools. This movement, pioneered by Macpherson and Percy Scholes, aimed to teach people to listen intelligently to music with the help of analytical study.

Listening tends to be confused with appreciation. Musical appreciation is broadly accepted to mean playing records or tapes to provide an introduction to a wider range of music (usually works of the 'great masters'); listening would aim to cover the same ground but may consider other aspects, for example as already stated, to develop an awareness of the environment.

Listening, appreciation, however it is referred to, is an area of music which until recently has been isolated from other activities and invariably badly taught. Rather than stimulating an interest in a wider range of music, it has often produced the opposite effect and succeeded in closing the minds of pupils. This is often a consequence of the teacher emphasising the analytical process supported by a large dose of historical detail, as being the best way of understanding music. A large proportion of the school population leave with not only an impression, but a firm view, that the music of Bach, Beethoven and Bartok is school music, the music of the teacher; they are led to believe that analysis, style and historical background are more important than the music itself.

Analysis and verbal discussion are concerned with knowing about rather than understanding music and there is no evidence to show that knowing about music ever leads to an understanding (Chapter 8, pp. 71–2). On the contrary, it would appear that verbalizing may prevent children from reaching a point of trying to understand. Music is a unique non-verbal language; therefore it follows that real understanding can only occur when it is permitted to communicate through its own language rather than by attempting to translate it into words. Explanations often remove the actual experience one stage further away from the individual; it can also be argued that music transmits feelings and sensations which are incapable of being translated adequately into words.

Some teachers use appreciation as a basis for all music teaching and preface their music syllabus with aims such as 'to introduce pupils to music of lasting value' or 'to promote an understanding of good music through a constructive listening programme'. This presupposes that because music has stood the test of time it must be good and conversely anything of recent origin can as yet have little value. There is additionally the problem of defining what is good; the teacher has to rely on her own taste to decide what is to be introduced to the pupils, a taste formed by her own experiences over a period of time. The teacher, hopefully, will have sampled a wide variety of music and as a consequence be able to lead the pupils rather than attempt to indoctrinate a blinkered view. Listening is such a personal matter that it would be wrong for the teacher to assume that pupils will react to music in the same way as she does, but her role may be seen as one of providing a wide range of listening for sampling purposes from which a pupil's interest and taste may further develop, for example by introducing music ranging from medieval to *Sequenza III* by Berio.

Commercial salesmen know only too well that by sampling, an individual is more likely to buy. Until wine is tasted and tried, it is unlikely that an individual will find a wine to suit his particular palate; there is always the chance that he might discover a suitable one by random choice, but unless many are sampled, the ability to be selective is made more difficult. If sampling is to be effective, the teacher may have to overcome her own prejudices and seek advice from others concerning music which does not appeal to her. The areas likely to fall into this category are those which experience has proved are the areas most likely to appeal to children, namely music of the 20th century ranging from Stockhausen to rock.

Many schools embark on inflexible listening programmes based on the assumption that as pupils grow older, they should be introduced to longer works and more complex formal structures; for example, in the first year binary and ternary form and by the third year, sonata form, symphony and concerto. Sometimes in a syllabus, composers are treated in chronological order commencing with Bach and Handel before reaching Schubert and Beethoven by the third year. Consequently pupils rarely reach the music of this century, having been satiated with the 17th, 18th and 19th and an array of concertos, sonatas, symphonies and operas, a pattern which links directly with many of the courses designed for music students in higher education or 'conservatoire' training.

Artists have the ability to see works of art, paintings, sculptures, buildings as a whole before looking at detail; this by and large is how children view music, but many musicians, as a result of conditioning, find it difficult to apply this principle and resort to dissection first; they are trained to mistrust instincts and feelings and thereafter seek to do the same with the pupils they teach.

To break down a motor engine into pieces and then reassemble it will help the individual to understand how the engine works and develops its power, but as a result would that person enjoy the ride any more? The working parts of music, the rhythm, melody and form, can also be taken apart but they themselves are only subsidiary, the means by which feelings and ideas are communicated. No matter how systematically they are broken down and reassembled, they are still not the real matter, the part which can in no way be analyzed. Reaction to music must be a personal one which no other individual will ever experience in the same way.

It may be argued that education is concerned with helping pupils to see matters from different viewpoints, and that the analytical process is another way of gaining understanding which might appeal to a pupil who responds to a logical approach. This is acceptable providing that the teacher misleads neither herself nor the pupil into believing that this leads to a real and deep understanding of music. Analysis may be helpful and indeed essential, for example, when a pupil has created a piece of music as a direct result of being stimulated by a listening experience, he may return to analyze certain aspects of the original in order to refine his own composition.

Is it too loud?

'Turn it down' is the plea often made by parents to their offspring. Why do many people enjoy listening to music at a high rate of decibels? Despite the general impression, it is not only the young who prefer to listen to music in this way, neither has it anything to do with a person being either sensitive, insensitive or being a trained musician or otherwise. There is little doubt that loud music can produce an emotional experience and is another way in which music communicates. This trend arose from pop music and developed through the use of non-acoustic instruments such as electric guitars. During the

1950s, pop groups began to use amplifiers of relatively small output (30 watts), but the development of solid state circuitry has led to the point where at a public rock concert literally thousands of watts are emitted from a vast array of equipment. There would be little point in listening very quietly to the climax of say, Ravel's *Bolero*, because the whole impact of what the music is trying to communicate would be lost. Rock music is intended to be played loudly; this is part of the way in which it communicates. Without volume it would lose much of its impact in the same way that low level (quiet) listening would detract from a Wagnerian climax. A feature of rock orientated music is that generally the sound level is loud and continuous. High levels of sound can cause physical pain, although the individual's ability to absorb volume differs from one person to another. Acceptable levels change through conditioning, for example, a person may enter a disco when the music is apparently excessively loud to the extent of causing pain, but if that person were to be admitted while sound levels were lower, she would most likely, after a period of gradual adjustment, be able to accept the original distressing level, this time without feeling any pain.

Why is loud music expected in discos and why do people endure it? What form does the experience take for the listener? The combination of regular rhythm and a high level of sound which can be felt to transmit vibrations through both floor and walls goes on to reach the point where it appears to take over the human body in the same way. This may be the experience which people seek; total identification of mind and body with sound. Reaction may take the form of hypnotic trance, and dance may appear close to frenzied tribal ritual. People not only escape from the world around them in this situation but allow music to communicate freely and they react accordingly without inhibition. The power music displays in reaching emotions can never be underestimated; it communicates feelings and sensations which words are neither capable of inducing nor adequate to describe.

Listening to loud music for a long period of time may damage the hearing permanently. The next decade is likely to reveal an alarming number of people who, through constant exposure to very loud music during adolescence and beyond, have brought about the onset of deafness to some degree much earlier in life than is necessary. Health education programmes in schools neglect this important aspect and would do well to inform young people of the dangers of this type of aural pollution. In an article by David Black in the Musicians' Union

Journal, *The Musician* (April 1981), 'Does Loud Music Make You Deaf?', he makes the point that hearing loss can take 5–25 years to show itself. A musician and health education officer, Black argues that 'although there are difficulties in deciding on length of exposure, repeated exposure to high levels of music can be damaging'. It has been suggested that musicians exposed for some 18 hours a week 'far exceed the risk level'. The same applies of course to those who spend many leisure hours listening to tapes and records, particularly to those who are subjected to a noisy daytime environment. Perhaps music teachers should also ensure that pupils are at least aware of the dangers and the possible long term consequences.

Knowledge or Understanding?

Whilst we must not forget that listening is an important part of all musical activities, the major concern for most teachers is the selection and presentation of listening material such as records and tapes. As has already been stated, actual selection is a personal matter, but teachers should ensure a wide choice and one which contains a significant proportion of music from this century and from today in particular. In actual presentation, teachers should remember to ensure that children have the opportunity to hear the material initially without being impeded. To develop an understanding of the music, repetition is essential at various intervals of time and the teacher may then find it useful to provide listening points, for example a theme written on the blackboard or a graphic score on an overhead projector. Listening may be an activity which stands on its own but could be used as a stimulus for composition. On the negative side, teachers should beware of using music as a stimulus for word writing or even painting. The difficulty in translating music into words has already been noted and similar problems exist for translating into other artistic activities. If the lesson is art- or English-based and the intention is to provide a stimulus for painting or creative writing, then the situation is different because music is used to stimulate other activity, but in the music lesson the prime concern is with music and the understanding of music through its own language. Music may stimulate thought and feelings in other languages, but is not directly translatable as many believe.

One final point – teachers sometimes follow a listening experience by giving pupils notes to write about the music. Arguments used to support this exercise are that it will help them to remember the music;

that children enjoy writing notes and collecting facts; and more to the point, if the school examines in all subject areas, that facts are immediately examinable. Suffice it to say without repeating arguments, that all these statements are concerned with knowledge as opposed to understanding. Does it matter whether a child remembers historical detail about the *Rite of Spring* by Stravinsky? There is no suggestion here that music is a non-examinable subject, but teachers must look closely at what it is they are trying to do. Art in education overcomes this problem by identifying the factual part as Art History while the core of the curriculum remains creatively based and is examined as such.

WHO NEEDS TO READ MUSIC?

This question is one of concern to many music teachers. A professional musician who makes a living by playing in an orchestra certainly needs to be able to read music, and one who plays in a pop/rock band may find it a useful skill, if an inessential one. Children who learn to play the piano or any orchestral instrument need to read music, firstly because without a reading facility a vast amount of repertoire will remain closed to the player; secondly because of the need to experience, for orchestral players, group activities and thirdly because instrumental teachers by and large teach through the eye rather than the ear.

Of the small number of people who read music fluently, it is safe to say that 99.9% develop this skill through playing an instrument or by singing regularly in a choral group. Approximately 10% of the school population have instrumental lessons and of these a very small proportion will go on to become professionals; the remainder will never need to read music or play instruments that demand this facility. It becomes increasingly difficult therefore to justify the amount of time which some teachers devote in the classroom to developing this skill, particularly where it is done in an abstract manner, that is, removed from the actual sound. Notation is a code, a way of recording music on paper so that it may be reproduced by others. Many musicians have believed that the key to music is the ability to read, but the development of practical music-making in its widest sense within the last few decades has finally put paid to this point of view. Seen as an aid, it begins to assume its true perspective.

All children will need to know something of notation, but that is significantly different from reading music. They will want to use appropriate notation for composition in some cases, although the cassette recorder mostly fulfils this function. How successful pupils are in accurately notating their intentions on paper may be put to the test by asking a second group to interpret the score, thereby measuring the effectiveness of the graphics.

Which notation should be introduced? The conventional notation which uses crotchets and quavers has proved to be ideal for European musical traditions within the last few centuries but at the same time its use in 20th century music has been restricted – partly by its inability to cope with technological developments both instrumentally and electronically. Much freer use of graphics has taken place in such circumstances and pupils will need to be encouraged to develop their own particular form of these according to the type of compositional work they are undertaking.

It is often argued that pupils who go on to take public examinations such as the General Certificate of Education (GCE) or its equivalent may be penalized as a result of not learning conventional notation in the classroom. Bearing in mind that the music examinations are taken by a small minority, as has already been said, it would be wrong to design a curriculum over a period of five years which provided only for the needs of this group. All pupils taking the examinations should have instrumental ability and their reading skills will have developed naturally through this experience.

Reading music means different things to different people; to some it may simply be the ability to follow the shape of a melody and work out the value of the notes, but to the professional it could mean being able to look at music and interpret it instantly on sight. There are obviously many variables, although a lot of mystique has been attached to this particular skill. The basic rudiments are easy to grasp but the ability to read fluently will only develop through constant practical involvement, and, even so, the standard likely to be achieved will vary. Most people read English fluently because of regular practice and simply in order to survive in a verbally orientated society; conversely few people read and speak French unless it is appropriate for their particular needs.

QUALITIES SOUGHT BY EMPLOYERS

Finally in this chapter, some of the qualities sought by employers are mentioned as a further justification for the music curriculum which has been outlined.

Schools are coming under increasing criticism not only from disenchanted school leavers but also from prospective employers. A group of teachers seconded for a year to an Understanding British Industry project in Birmingham in the late 1970s, identified nine of the major qualities sought by employers. It was revealed in discussion with leaders of this group that, of all curriculum subjects, music was, in many schools, the only area contributing to the majority of the requirements. The nine points were summarized as:

1. The ability to work quickly and accurately.
2. The development of good written and aural communication skills.
3. The need to be flexible, adaptable, and willing to accept change.
4. Possession of mathematical, spatial and computational skills.
5. Well developed motor-skills.
6. Possession of self-awareness and the ability and confidence to make decisions.
7. The ability to co-operate. Employers were critical of teachers for constantly discouraging co-operation. Too often 'talking together' was seen as a disruptive activity, whereas work outside school usually involved a great deal of team work.
8. The ability to be creative/inventive and to possess initiative.
9. The desire to do a good job, to conclude it and to share it with others.

Unemployment, or the likelihood of it, is the concern of most young people at this time, but nevertheless too many are leaving school ill-equipped for either employment or unemployment. The qualities described above would in general terms be appropriate for either situation and teachers may well find it a profitable exercise to ensure that the points are embraced within the curriculum.

CONCLUSION

The aim of this chapter has been to provide the music teacher with some thoughts and ideas for constructing a curriculum and translating it into the written word for all to see. Once this has been achieved, teaching becomes more purposeful; the English education system enables individuals to create their own curriculum to the advantage of all concerned.

REFERENCES

Beatles, *The Beatles Complete*, Wm. H. Wise/Music Sales, Union City, N.J.
Berio, *Sequenza*, Universal, 1968.
Black, D., 'Does Loud Music Make You Deaf?', *The Musicians' Union Journal*, April 1981.
Blyton, C., *Konrad of the Mountains*, Music Workshop Stage 2, BBC, 1969.
Brace, G., *Something to Sing*, C.U.P., 1976.
Brocklehurst, B., *Pentatonic Song Book*, Schott, 1968.
Chappell, H., *The Daniel Jazz*, Novello, 1963.
Crosse, G., *Ahmet the Woodseller*, O.U.P., 1965.
Flanders, M. and Horovitz, J., *Captain Noah and His Floating Zoo*, Novello, 1970.
Hurd, M., *Jonah Man Jazz*, Novello, 1967.
Lloyd Webber, A., *Joseph and the Amazing Technicolour Dreamcoat*, Novello, 1967.
Paynter, E. and J., *The Dance and the Drum*, Universal, 1974.
Play it again and again and again series, Chappell, 1981.
Schools Council, *Music and the Young School Leaver: Problems and Opportunities*, Working Paper 35, Evans/Methuen, 1971.
Simon, P. and Garfunkel, A., *Simon and Garfunkel's Greatest Hits*, Pattern/Music Sales, 1968.
Winters, G., *Drake's Voyage*, O.U.P., 1970.
101 Hits for Buskers series, Wm. H. Wise/Music Sales, Union City, N.J.

SUGGESTED FURTHER READING

Arnold, J., *The Organisation of Small-Group Work in the Classroom*, Schools Council, University of York, 1980.
Johnson, R. (Ed.), *An Anthology of New Music*, Schirmer, 1981.
Paynter, J., *Hear and Now* (an introduction to modern music in schools), Universal, 1972.
Price, E., 'Repertory: Group Music', *Music in Education*, February, 1978.
Swanwick, K. and Taylor, D., *Discovering Music*, Batsford, 1982.

SUGGESTED SONGS/VOCAL RESOURCES

Attwood, T., *Pop Song Books*, O.U.P., 1981.
Brace, G., *Something to Sing* series, C.U.P., 1965.
Brocklehurst, B., *Pentatonic Song Book*, Schott, 1968.
Christian, Burnett, *Reggae Schooldays*, EMI, 1982.
    Caribbean Adventure, EMI, 1981.
Dobbs, J., Fiske, R., Lane M., *Ears and Eyes* series, O.U.P., 1974.
Gadsby, D. and Harrop, B., *Flying Around*, A. and C. Black, 1982.
Horton, J., *The Music Group* series, Schott, 1969.
Jenkins, and Visocchi, *Mix 'N Match*, Universal, 1977.
    More Mix 'N Match, Universal, 1979.
Lorentzen, B., *New Choral Dramatics*, Walton, New York, 1971.
Milne, L., *The Fix-It Man*, Macmillan, 1979.
Paynter, J., *All Kinds of Music* series, O.U.P., 1976.
Stevens, S., *Swing Along Songs*, EMI, 1981.

Norell, T. and Wahlberg, U., *Popcorn*, C.U.P., 1980.
Wishart, T., *Sounds Fun*, musical games, Schools Council, University of York, 1975.
    Sounds Fun 2, Universal, 1977.

INSTRUMENTAL/SOUND PROJECTS

Attwood, T. and Farmer, P., *Pop Workbook*, Edward Arnold, 1978.
Bissell, K., *Let's Sing and Play*, Waterloo, 1975.
Dennis, B., *Experimental Music in Schools*, O.U.P., 1970.
    Projects in Sound, Universal, 1975.
ILEA, *Sounds Together*, 1980.
    Sounds Unlimited, 1980.
    Choosing and Using Classroom Instruments, 1980.
Inner London Education Authority, Teachers Music Centre, Sutherland Street, London SW1.
Lichfield, P., *Classroom Pieces in a Variety of Styles*, Midland Centre for Music in Schools, City of Birmingham Polytechnic, Westbourne Rd., Birmingham B15 3TN, 1983.
Music for Young Players series (contemporary instrumental and vocal pieces), Universal.
Osborne, N., *Creative Projects* for middle school, Chappell, 1981.
Self, G., *New Sounds in Class*, Universal Edition (London) Ltd., 1967.
    Make a New Sound, Universal Edition (London) Ltd., 1976.
Tillman, J., *Exploring Sound*, Stainer & Bell, 1976.
Ways with Music series, Chappell.
Walker, R., *Sound Projects*, O.U.P., 1970.

ELECTRONIC MUSIC

Anderton, C., *Electronic Projects for Musicians*, Guitar Player Productions, 1975.
Drake, R., Herder, R., Modugno, A.D., *How to Make Electronic Music*, Audio Visual Inc./Harmony Books, 1975.
Duncan, T., *Adventures with Electronics*, John Murray, 1978.
Dwyer, T., *Composing with Tape Recorders*, O.U.P., 1971.
    Making Electronic Music series, O.U.P.
Gardner, J., *Creative Tape Recording*, Newnes, 1977.
Mowers, T.D., *Electronics in Music*, Newnes, 1976.

MAKING INSTRUMENTS

Brune, J.A., *Resonant Rubbish*, English Folk Dance and Song Society, 1974.
Dankworth, A., *Voices and Instruments*, Hart-Davis Educational, 1973.
Mandell, M.E. and Wood, R.E., *Make Your Own Musical Instruments*, Bailey/Sterling, New York, 1970.
Romney, E., *The Musical Instrument Recipe Book*, Penguin Education, 1974.

CHAPTER TEN

Evaluation and Assessment
... for teachers

During the past few decades schools have generally moved from formal teaching methods to what may be described as more freely structured learning experiences. The pressure has always been on teachers to keep up to date with trends and methods, but often with little thought as to how children's work emerging from these might be evaluated and assessed. Evaluation obviously does take place in the teacher's mind, but the constant call for accountability from both parents and government demands that the actual process of evaluation and assessment of children's work in all subject areas must be seen to be done and be recorded in a positive and tangible way.

Schools do evaluate the various aspects of curriculum by looking to see whether aims have been achieved through the various objectives and content prescribed, but in this instance the concern is for evaluating and assessing the work produced by pupils.

Evaluating children's work can be a relatively simple task when the main objective of the curriculum has been to impart knowledge; by giving a test, written or oral, it is easy to assess whether pupils have learnt a particular piece of information. For example, with mathematics it may be a straightforward process to discover whether children have mastered the technique of mechanically solving a problem, but it is not so easy to establish whether they have understood the concept behind it.

Many secondary schools organize examinations in all subjects once or twice a year and this may force the music teacher into a difficult situation. Some take the view that unless music takes its place alongside other subjects in such an exercise, it will be seen as being less important in the eyes of both pupils and staff; so in order to gain artificial prestige, these teachers submit pupils to information testing.

A number of teachers think that music in education should display 'academic rigour' in order to be taken seriously, and they generally assume that the curriculum will contain a substantial proportion of information being taught, received and regurgitated. These are easy options, and steering a curriculum in this way to feed the internal examination system would be difficult to justify in educational terms. Other music teachers are of the opinion that examinations are a permanent blight which has to be faced, and therefore they ensure that testing genuinely reflects learning experiences and modes of teaching in the curriculum.

An example of this latter type of examination would be:

Composition
Submission of a mini-portfolio containing two or three pieces completed during the year. The portfolio may consist of live performance of compositions, tape recordings or written scores of pieces.
Practical
Assessment in performance individually or as part of a group, either in the classroom or in extra-timetable activities, for example:

    a. performing compositions.
    b. solo instrumental or vocal performance.
    c. as a member of choir, wind band or rock group.
Listening
Identifying musical styles, for example Bob Marley, Duke Ellington, Britten, and identifying musical texture and colour.

The proposals for the new 16+ public examination due to be introduced in the next few years are well advanced but not finalized at the time of writing; it is likely that they will contain the elements listed above although they may not be examined in the suggested way.

As far as classroom activity is concerned, it is important to establish some broad criteria for evaluating and assessing the various activities, but the thorny one, the aspect to be considered here, is that of creative work. How is it possible to assess quality, originality or the ability to communicate through the language of music?

In the 'adult' world, a composer's music is measured only by the finished product, but in education how pupils travel through experiences and stages to arrive at a product is equally if not more important; for example how they discover sound potential from materials, how they organize the materials to express ideas or how they tackle the review and refinement process. One of the weaknesses of the examination system is that in general it takes account only of the summative experience and does not acknowledge the value of the learning process itself.

It might be useful to recall how musicians assess practical examinations. To assess accuracy of playing and therefore technique is relatively easy but to assess interpretative qualities and ability to communicate through music are other matters. Musicians can do this and by and large find little difficulty in establishing broad agreement as to performers' qualities in this respect, although defining the qualities verbally is difficult. Musicians in fact do evaluate and assess as a result of their own experiences in music built up over a period of time, but whereas most musicians are performers to some degree, fewer are composers, and applying appropriate criteria based on personal experience may therefore be impossible.

To award a mark for original work is an unenviable task. Ideally those placed in this situation will have experienced the composition process for themselves at some level. Perhaps this is too much to expect from all primary school teachers, but they are the only people who are in a position to take account of the complete creative process undergone by the pupils in their charge. A teacher working with a class from day to day will quickly become aware of development, facility in handling materials, the ability to organize, express and structure ideas, and this may be adequate; nevertheless it is desirable that any teacher undertaking the role of a specialist in either primary or secondary school should have had personal experience of composition.

Tape recordings are essential evidence of what each pupil has produced, if only to demonstrate to outsiders the development of the child, but they can also serve as a useful recall for a teacher when it comes to producing an overall evaluation or assessment, especially when there is no examination.

So the evaluation and assessment of classroom composition work may be identified as being approached from three directions:

(a) Evaluation of the process which leads to the product.
(b) The pupil's evaluation and assessment of her own work.
(c) Assessment of the product.

The following list of questions should help to establish a basis for evaluation and assessment in this difficult area.

(a) Evaluating the Process

1. How did the pupil respond to the 'sensate' problem set by the teacher if indeed there was one?
2. Has full and imaginative use been made of the materials and facilities available?
3. Have the necessary practical skills for this piece been developed?
4. How far has the review and refinement process been used? Has the pupil shown ability and persistence to reassess and rewrite in order to produce a more polished product and see the work complete as far as possible?
5. Is the ability to express ideas through the language of music showing signs of development?

(b) The Pupil's Own Evaluation and Assessment

Information required: Name of piece, date started and completed, duration of performance.

1. Describe the task set and by whom.
2. How far have you kept to this or deviated from it?
3. What resources are used?
4. How did you record the piece?
5. Is live performance possible?
6. Describe how you constructed the piece.
7. Does it have shape or form?
8. How did you decide which sounds to use?
9. Is the piece too short or too long?
10. Is it too complex or simple?
11. What are its best moments?
12. What is the weakest part?
13. Have you succeeded in capturing the mood you set out to achieve?
14. Are you satisfied with the final product? If not why not?
15. How does this piece compare with your previous one? Is it better or not as good? Can you say why?
16. Was it a group composition? If so what did each person contribute?
17. Assess the piece in terms of a grade, either A, B, C, D, or E.
18. Have you any idea what your next piece will be?

(c) Assessing the Product

This particular part of the assessment is inevitably subjective but will be greatly assisted by assimilating both the process (a) and the pupil's evaluation of the product (b). In the opinion of the teacher:

1. Does the composition achieve what it set out to do?
2. Is it concise, rambling, too short or too long?
3. Is it too complex or is it simple?
4. Does it have shape or form and is this successfully handled?
5. Does it communicate?
6. Is the recording of adequate standard?
7. Whether live or recorded, does it have 'feel'?
8. Does it make sense?
9. Is it original, or pastiche?
10. What is the style of language used and has it changed from previous pieces?
11. Has there been imaginative use of resources?
12. How does it compare as a whole with the previous piece?
13. Is there evidence of progress, growing maturity and confidence in composition?

Although pupils are often reluctant to talk about their compositions and often simply want to get on with the next, nevertheless the value of involving them in a self-assessment exercise cannot be underestimated. Depending on the pupil, this might take the form of a written self-assessment in answer to the questions provided or could be a verbal discussion between pupil and teacher around the issues described. It would be more suitable to introduce the latter method for primary school children, but whenever used the conversation should be tape recorded and kept together with a cassette of the performance. Constant use of tape recorders in the composition process will ensure that pupils are quite content for information to be recorded and stored in this way. The timing of administering this self-assessment could be critical and the teacher will have to decide when is appropriate for each individual; it could take place immediately or some weeks later depending on the need of the pupil to pursue other tasks.

The combination of the information and opinions arising from the three areas of evaluation and assessment should allow a teacher to arrive at some form of assessment if required. It will mean more written work for the teacher but duplicated proformas could easily be used. The evaluation and assessment document should be seen by the pupils and the information may then be retained together with a copy of the tape/manuscript in a pupil's profile folder for parents and others to see. The fact that the process as well as the product is part of the overall evaluation and assessment will reassure pupils who may fear assessment of the product itself in isolation by a teacher/examiner who is out of sympathy with their particular product.

The suggested form of evaluation and assessment should be experimented with and amended according to the needs of particular schools, age of pupils and curriculum content offered.

The question of arts assessment is one which a number of groups are attempting to research. The APU (Assessment of Performance Unit) has recently published a discussion document, *Aesthetic Development* (1983), and as the title implies it concentrates on the assessment of artistic development. So the ideas put forward in this chapter may be considered as a useful, practical stop gap until such time as more empirically researched evidence becomes available.

REFERENCES

APU, *Aesthetic Development*, Department of Education and Science, London, 1983.
Gulbenkian, *The Arts in Schools*, Gulbenkian Foundation, 1982.
Schools Council Project, *Music in the Secondary School Curriculum*, University of York, 1973–80.
    Bryan, J. (Ed.), *Process or Product: the Evaluation of Artistic Achievement*, Course Paper 1, 1976.
    Bunting, R. (Ed.), *Personal–Practical–Topical*, Working Paper 2, 1975.
    Paynter, J., *The Evaluation of Classroom Music Activities*, Parts 1 and 2, Working Paper 4, 1977.

SUGGESTED FURTHER READING

Department of Education and Science, *Assessing the Performance of Pupils*, Report No. 93, HMSO, 1978.
Open University, 'Examinations and Assessment', *Contemporary issues in Education*, Booklet E200, 1981.
Wiseman, S. and Pedgeon, D., *Curriculum Evaluation*, NFER, 1970.

CHAPTER ELEVEN
Beyond the Timetable
. . . activities for all

Extra-curricular music activities are those which take place either during lunch break or before/after the normal school timetable.

These activities are thought by many music teachers to be the most important part of their work; paradoxically, they are viewed by a large number of teachers of other subjects and parents as being merely peripheral to the real areas of learning. There is, however, little doubt that they have an important part to play in the growth of experience and overall development of many pupils, especially those who play musical instruments. If this is so, the term extra-curricular is inappropriate – it should be *extra-timetable*.

The fact that the activities are extra-timetable indicates that pupils attend voluntarily and are presumably interested in music-making. For this reason, many specialists concentrate their energies on working with these pupils at the expense of compulsory class lesson activity where the challenge may be greater. Because activities take place after school, there is competition for the interests of the pupils; the most skilled musician is likely to be an able chess player, a useful sportswoman or a key member of some other organisation which meets at the same time on the same day. Experiments have been made to include some activities within the general timetable to overcome such problems, but with limited success. Unless options are open to a wide number of pupils at a particular time, the only alternative would be to draw pupils out of lessons, a situation which has generally proved to be unacceptable to pupils, teachers and their parents. So, if experience has shown that in most schools these activities are best organized as an extension of the school day, then it is desirable that they should be acknowledged by being shown on an extended school timetable. The Newsom report, *Half Our Future* (1963), recommended that extra-curricular activities ought to be recognised as an integral part of the total education programme, and secured where necessary by administrative provision. Several things follow: first, the school programme needs to be envisaged as a whole, with 'curricular' and 'extra-curricular' activities planned as complementary parts. Secondly, the school day should be conceived as extending beyond the nine-til-four limits.

The aims of these activities can be seen as:

1. to provide an extension of opportunity for all pupils to develop individual interests and abilities –
2. to ensure that those pupils having instrumental lessons are given the opportunity to take part in ensemble work –
and as a result if so desired –
3. to provide a series of informal/formal performances.

The pattern of activities in any one school is obviously dictated by staff interests, particular needs and interests of pupils and to a certain extent by traditions long established. For example, certain schools have reputations for specializing in a specific activity, perhaps exceptional choral work, or are renowned for outstanding work in the brass band field. Some examples of existing programmes are given below.

School A

1600 pupils – 3 full-time music teachers

School A follows the tradition of presenting one major concert/ performance each term, which includes the larger scale activities such as choir and orchestra and also attempts to include some of the other performing groups.

Music is an important feature of the daily school assembly with the emphasis on choral work, but orchestra, wind band, gospel choir, folk group, recorder ensemble and steel band contribute at least once each every three weeks. Other groups, such as the rock bands, also make appearances as and when appropriate. The school aims for high standards in all performing activities and it believes that the regular sharing of experiences at the daily assembly not only contributes to maintaining this standard, but also generates an enthusiasm and 'respect' for music both in the classroom and outside.

In the Autumn term, the major event is the Christmas music/Carol

	8.00 a.m. before school time-table	LUNCH-TIME Teacher			Un-staffed	AFTER SCHOOL Teacher			Un-staffed
		A	B	C		A	B	C	
Monday	MUSIC DEPARTMENT OPEN FOR PRACTICE AND ACTIVITIES AS REQUIRED; STAFF SUPERVISE ON A ROTA BASIS – ONE WEEK IN THREE		Junior Choir				Orch-estra		
Tuesday				Elec-tronic Work-shop	Folk Group	Steel Band	Wind Band		
Wednesday		Junior Orchestra					Full Choir		
Thursday		Improvi-sation Group		Recor-der En-semble			Swing Band		Gospel Choir
Friday					Rock and Pop Bands				Pop and Rock Bands

concert, which includes choir, orchestra, wind band and as many of the smaller groups as is practical; essentially it is an event where as many performers as possible work together with a single aim in view.

The Spring term brings about an attempt to pool the resources of the larger groups. Recently a longer work was attempted which included all singers, some players and a group of singers from a local church choir. The piece in question was Benjamin Britten's *Saint Nicolas*.

In the Summer term a concert performance of *Joseph and the Amazing Technicolour Dreamcoat* was presented; the remainder of the programme included pop song arrangements for singers and players, wind band, swing band and the best of the pop and rock groups.

Some of the other performance activities which took place during the year, with assistance from other members of staff, included visits at Christmas time to local hospitals, old people's homes and to the local shopping precinct. In the summer, the school fete and local community carnival celebrations provided further opportunities. The gospel choir entered a local choral competition, and in addition to performing at an in-service teachers' course, they extended their work into the local church communities. The folk group made a recording, the proceeds of which were donated partly to local charities and partly to school funds. Twice a term, the pop and rock bands play for a dance; usually sufficient material is available for a full evening's entertainment, but where not, continuity and support is provided by the school disco. The swing band, amongst other activities, played for a Parent/Teacher Association dance, with music from the 1940s to the 1960s.

Informal lunchtime concerts are vigorously encouraged, and each year during the last week of the summer term a series of concerts takes place daily during lesson time, largely built around individual and small group performances; pupils are particularly urged to present new music on these occasions. The timing within the school year ensures that teachers are prepared to release pupils wishing to attend these events.

Music is a driving force in this school and in one way or another it envelops all pupils; they simply cannot ignore it. This is not the place to embark on a discussion about the effect of music on general attitudes throughout the school in terms of behaviour or learning, but having considered the description of activity in School A, it is not difficult to grasp some idea of the sense of purpose and enthusiasm which greets any visitor to this particular school.

School B

1100 pupils – 2 full-time music teachers

This school undertakes a much reduced programme compared to School A. The music activities are geared to specific events and therefore large group rehearsals, for example choir and orchestra, lead up to concerts rather than take place on a weekly basis. The events are:

Autumn Term
Carols/Christmas Music. These involve primarily the choir and various instrumental groups. Rehearsals commence in October.

Spring Term
Oliver (the previous year a Gilbert and Sullivan opera). The production is in March; rehearsals for soloists begin in October but for chorus and orchestra in January.

Summer Term

Inter-House Music Festival. No large scale activities take place during this term.

School C

1000 pupils – 2 full-time music teachers

The energies of the staff here are devoted to work in the classroom, and although encouragement is given to pupils who organize group activities, the staff do not direct any formal activities with one exception, the brass band. There has been a long tradition of brass work in this school and the band continues to give regular concerts, to take part in competitive festivals, to play for morning assembly and to be involved with the community beyond the school.

*   *   *   *

These are of course only three examples of what is taking place; there are endless variables. Concerts are occasions for drawing the general public into the school community and can become prestige events not only for the music teacher but for the pupils, headteacher and school as a whole. Performance is thought by many teachers to be important; it gives the opportunity to organize available talent to provide entertainment as well as to make it possible to measure the progress of individuals and to assess the quality of teaching. Performance encourages many pupils to attain peaks of achievement which they might never reach under other circumstances. Corporate achievement, for example within a large choir, may contribute to a welding together of the school community, and for the music teacher a successful concert can make life a good deal easier in terms of his standing in the eyes of both pupils and other teachers.

A substantial number of teachers, however, make the point that performance is unimportant and that it is the process leading up to a performance which benefits the pupils most. Others argue that many pupils do not enjoy performing in public and therefore should not be subjected to this form of 'torture'.

Whether performance be the end result or not, extra-timetable activities can be seen to be an important aspect of the school curriculum. The problem for each school is to arrive at a reasonable balance in terms of what can be achieved within the physical resources available. No teacher can be expected to work from 8.00 a.m., teach a full day's timetable, work through lunch hour and then direct an activity into the early evening. It is possible but only for a limited period in anyone's life.

INSTRUMENTAL ACTIVITIES

The growth of instrumental teaching over the last two or three decades has challenged the music teacher to provide a wide range of opportunities for all instrumentalists to be involved in ensemble work, a contrast to previous times when most schools' activities were purely choral.

The value of corporate work has already been touched on; pupils gain enjoyment from playing in a group with others and the satisfaction gained from using skills, however elementary or limited, to contribute to an ensemble, is a further encouragement for the pupil to continue with instrumental work. The social aspect should not be undervalued; one of the great pleasures in life for a musician is to make music with others, an activity which calls for understanding and acceptance of the weaknesses and strengths of those taking part, and yet within those limitations develop team work to overcome the problems posed by the music. A band or orchestra has to work as a team because all are aiming towards the same goal; within that team, it would depend on the personality of the director as to how much individual skill is allowed to contribute. Some directors adopt the role of absolute dictator, perhaps because they feel unsure, while others give players more freedom to interpret.

The music teacher has the never-ending problem of finding suitable music for players; the difficulty is caused by the different standards of the various individuals within the groups. Even where separate ensembles are organized for beginners, moderate and advanced players, within those groups there is still likely to be a wide range of ability. Unlike the professional orchestra where instrumental standard is of a minimum level, the music teacher has to organize groups containing whatever skills the pupils offer; so music has to be found which will not only cater for an assortment of individuals all with different levels of ability, but it has to be at the right level to promote further development at the same time. The problem is accentuated in smaller schools where a much wider range of ability has to be catered for within one ensemble because of reduced staffing especially if it is accepted that as soon as pupils can play a range of notes on an instrument, then some form of group work should be provided. The situation can and does arise where the teacher has to attempt to accommodate, for example, string players who can only cope with first position work and grade six or seven players within the same ensemble. The better player may easily become discontented and express a wish not to take part, or miss rehearsals surreptitiously, but if the group is to develop, it will depend on the ability of the more able to provide the impetus; it is the key players who set the standard. Many teachers will have met the pupil who considers himself to be too good for the school ensemble, perhaps because he has progressed into a regional youth band or orchestra where more is demanded; he may be the best player in the school group and therefore be intolerant of those with limited skill. More than one teacher has washed her hands of such a pupil, but it is worth remembering that in most cases, this is only a temporary problem and an attitude which most young players will experience. It will also help this particular type of situation if further opportunities in small ensembles are provided in order to stretch the player. For example, if the pupil is a violinist an attempt should be made to recruit others to form a string quartet. If there are insufficient players of a high enough standard within the school, then the teacher may turn to the outside community to form such a group.

The problem of searching for suitable music has already been mentioned. Music publishers market what are usually referred to as multi-purpose arrangements; these are suitable for any combination of instruments including strings, woodwind and brass, but do not necessarily cater for a wide range of ability. The numerous series available include those published by Boosey and Hawkes, Belwin Mills, Chappell and Chester.

The ideal alternative is for a music teacher to write material for her own players. It requires considerable skill to arrange for the beginner and advanced at the same time, but is essential if the aim is to provide for the individual needs of the players. Time is the major opponent of such a scheme, but teachers have found that eventually they become skilful at producing arrangements quickly. Once a small collection has been built up, then it is easy to adapt material for future use.

Accuracy in copying parts is important; there is nothing more frustrating for players or conductor than to spend a large proportion of rehearsal time trying to find out why a particular section of the arrangement does not work, simply because someone has left out a couple of bars whilst copying. Reference points must be added to the arrangement so that it is not necessary always to return to the beginning when rehearsing. Commercial publishers favour a letter system of A, B and so on, but experience has shown that to number the bars is the safest way of avoiding ambiguous rehearsal instructions. To be able to say 'start at bar 137' is much quicker and easier for all concerned than to say 'begin at 7 before letter C'.

Brass Band

A long-standing activity in English schools is the *brass band*, an activity which stemmed from the movement largely associated with the industrial areas of the north of England. For the music teacher who is a non-brass player, the whole movement tends be shrouded in mystery. Some musicians have also refused to take the movement seriously because of the impression that the repertoire consists of music of 'doubtful' taste. Opinions of this kind are of course inaccurate; the whole movement today is a vigorous and challenging organization. Respectability has been enhanced by the spate of serious compositions which have been written specifically for brass bands, frequently as a result of a commission for a competition test piece, for example music by Elgar Howarth. The competitions themselves have revealed to the general public the skill and virtuosity of many of the leading players. There also exists an international youth brass band organization which has influenced the growth and development of bands in many schools.

The element of mystery already referred to arises chiefly from two sources: first, the instruments used, trombones and tubas apart, are unique to the brass and military band. Tenor horns, baritones, euphoniums and the division of cornets into solo and ripieno all add to the confusion. The second matter concerns the actual notation or rather the transposition of parts. This again can lead to total bewilderment; all players including the bass instruments read music from the treble clef, a method presumably originating from the early times of the brass band movement, which permitted players to move from one instrument to another without having to learn to read a different clef or use different fingering for each instrument. It must be stressed that this is not a problem for the players but simply one which needs to be understood by those likely to come into contact with this work.

All brass instruments used are pitched either in B flat or E flat, but by transposing, the actual written parts are related to the key of C. For example, for a B flat instrument to actually sound B flat, the player would produce it in open position, that is without depressing any valves; on an E flat instrument, to obtain the note E flat, again it would be produced in open position. When it actually comes to writing the note sounding B flat for the B flat instrument, the method is to write the note C and for the E flat instrument to write the note C to produce the sound E flat. Therefore a player could pick up either a B flat or E flat instrument and without having to change fingering or read a different clef, play the written part, always providing of course that the embouchure allowed him to do so.

The repertoire is vast and it really is a matter of personal taste for each band director to select the direction to pursue. Many school bands use, for example, Stuart Johnson's *Brass Band Books* (R. Smith, 1970 and following) as a basis and supplement these with material from the many series available including those published by Chester and Boosey and Hawkes.

Concert/Wind Bands

A main area of growth in recent years has been that of the *wind band*, sometimes referred to as the concert band or even military band. Although marching and concert bands are the core of musical activity in many schools and colleges in the United States, here the wind band is a relative newcomer.

Many American schools and colleges organize the concert band on almost a team basis; players progress from one band to another until they reach the top band. In many schools it is regarded as a great honour to represent the institution in the best marching band, a situation where, for better or worse, the music curriculum revolves around the whole concert/marching band system. We have not reached a similar position here, nor are we likely to do so. The average school may assemble two wind bands, an elementary group which encourages beginners to take part in ensemble work almost as soon as they can play two or three notes, and a second larger group catering for a much wider range of ability. In view of the large number of wind players to be found, the wind band has an important role to play, because unlike its competitor, the school orchestra, it is able to absorb all wind players of diverse ability with apparent ease.

What is a wind band? The definition as understood in school, is an instrumental group relating to the military band, rather than the more limited group consisting of woodwind and horns, written for by

Mozart. It uses all woodwind instruments including the saxophone, most brass instruments, sometimes percussion, an occasional string bass and more recently with pop-influenced material, the bass guitar.

The distinctive sound produced by the wind band appears to be acceptable to most people; it is also an ensemble which adapts easily to a variety of music ranging from Rossini to Leroy Anderson. The repertoire is vast and consists largely of arrangements from many sources, from symphonic movements to selections from musicals or of pop songs, but unlike the brass band or the concert band movement in the United States little original music of any substance is being written. Of the English material available, the compositions of Gustav Holst are among the best. The two suites, *No. 1 in E flat* (1909) and *No. 2 in F* (Boosey and Hawkes, 1911) are timeless classics; both are inspired by English folksong and are written for the conventional military band instrumentation. Holst was a master at writing for this combination although his other substantial work *Hammersmith* (Boosey and Hawkes, 1930), a mystical masterpiece, is difficult to play. The *English Folk Song Suite* by Vaughan Williams (Boosey and Hawkes, 1923) is well known and again finds its way into most band libraries. Gordon Jacob has also made a substantial contribution to the repertoire and is admired for his imaginative orchestration.

Material at all levels is available from many publishers including Novello, Oxford University Press, Belwin Mills, Rubank and Chappell.

Swing Bands/Stage Bands

A more recent development which is coupled with a revived interest in general in the music of the 1930s to 1950s, is that of the big band sound, which appeals to young musicians in schools. The usual line-up is a rhythm section consisting of piano, bass, drums, and if available, rhythm guitar plus six/eight brass normally including three/four trumpets and the same number of trombones, complemented by five saxophones, usually two alto, two tenor and a baritone. The saxophones, like the brass band instruments, all play from the treble clef and the same principles of transposition apply. There are many variations of the combinations described, depending on the players available and the music to be played; for example, the more complex arrangements used by Stan Kenton may demand five trumpets and five trombones. Schools can and often do begin with a much reduced line-up; there is a large amount of music available for virtually any combination, but the band leader will have to turn to American publications for anything resembling a band method which caters for development of the players in an organized way. That apart, it is a somewhat hit and miss affair if the music teacher has had no experience in this particular area of playing. Most semi-professional bands carry a set of arrangements which are readable at sight, and the music teacher would do well to look at one of these libraries if ideas are needed for repertoire, or simply go and listen to one of the many 'rehearsal bands' which now exist.

Band libraries are usually organized into 'pads' for each instrument, folders containing on average between 400 and 600 pieces. Most of these are referred to as *standards*, but other arrangements which also tend to be printed on larger size paper are called *specials*; standards are usually playable by almost any combination from a quartet upwards to a full band with parts cued in. Band libraries in the past tended to contain a large number of *Lallys*, functional but easily playable arrangements turned out by a prolific writer, Jimmy Lally. Many of the standard arrangements are perfectly acceptable for the inexperienced band to cope with, but they generally lack stimulating material. There are exceptions, but the more advanced band will have to look for suitable specials which range from fairly easy arrangements of pop to the very difficult Sammy Nestico/Count Basie material. Obviously to build a library is an expensive matter. For the type of arrangements which will work with any combination, it is worth contacting the local office of the Musicians' Union, or keeping a watchful eye on the for sale columns in the local newspaper; band libraries do become available at very reasonable prices. The Musicians' Union has done much to promote availability of inexpensive duplicated material for experienced bands under the heading of the *Stanza* series.

The availability of players may cause problems for the teacher who is organizing a band for the first time in a school. Brass players are usually looking eagerly for such an opportunity but finding saxophone players may be a more difficult matter. Apart from wind band playing where saxophone parts are not always the most imaginative, there is little scope to become involved with ensemble work outside the big band. This uniqueness tends to limit the number of players available and poses a real problem when trying to establish a group of five players who will blend together as a unit. Saxophone sections need specialized coaching in matters of style and phrasing; an experienced semi-professional or professional big band player will, by example, help the section to grasp these matters and particularly the problem of interpreting written rhythms. Certain patterns are approached in quite a different way from the conventional 'straight' way of playing; for example, dotted rhythms are usually played almost as triplet divisions:

$$\musical{} \quad becomes \quad \musical{}$$

It is more a question of feeling the style, which in time becomes instinctive.

A good drummer is essential, not necessarily one who has developed a lot of technique, but one who can maintain a steady rhythm. Drummers talk in terms of 'driving the band', that is, inspiring the players to give that little bit extra, but it takes time for this ability to develop.

Fluent double bass players are not often available, but most large schools have one pupil who has some ability on the bass guitar. The tendency in the professional band world is to use this in preference to the double bass not only because of its transportability, but partly because it provides a firmer foundation for the band and it can modify its sound level as appropriate. In the pop world the bass guitar has become a 'front-line' instrument and therefore if a big band proposes to include arrangements of up to date material, then the need for the guitar is apparent.

Pianists are usually available within a school, but even in the professional world it is not always easy to find a player who can adapt readily to a style which is foreign to conventional piano playing. Again there is a tendency to use electric pianos in rhythm sections.

Bands seem to be getting louder; brass players have little difficulty in matching the general level of increase in sound, but during a performance saxophones require some form of amplification to correct the balance. Too many bands play too loudly for too much of the time, but perhaps this is also a modern trend.

To be able to improvise is a useful asset in big band playing; even at a professional level, many section men do not consider themselves to be good improvisers. Young people will certainly need help to develop this facility; again structured programmes from the American market are available, for example, Dominic Spera's *Jazz Improvisation Series* (Hal Leonard, 1975). Many players have their first experience of improvising by working out simple riffs, usually short melodic figures which may link together phrases from the main tune. These are committed to memory and used as a basis for building improvisations. Other players base their first attempts at improvisation around the basic arpeggios surrounding the chord structure of a given song.

Within a band, it is customary to organize smaller combinations of players or *combos*. A dixieland group is popular because it caters literally for the best player in each section and is a contrast to the big band sound.

Band leaders ought not to forget that the human voice has immediate appeal and any programme should include some vocals backed by the band if at all possible.

OTHER ACTIVITIES

As can be seen, particularly from the example of School A, many other small group activities exist according to the particular interests of pupils and staff. Forming a steel band may be daunting prospect to some teachers, but if this is a proposed activity, reference should be made to the book list at the end of this chapter.

Choral activities have become wider in scope and nowadays include a proliferation of smaller selective groups often reflecting the multi-ethnic school population. These particular groups tend to select their own material and develop their individual style of performance with little assistance required from music staff, for example, the gospel choir will inevitably arise from church activities of a number of pupils but also grow to envelop others from the school community.

Keep Music Live is a slogan used by the Musicians' Union. Live music activities as part of the school curriculum make a contribution towards counteracting the canned and 'plasticized' musical diet which is being fed in ever increasing proportions to the population. The tragedy is that too few pupils carry their practical interests through to adult life, but until education is no longer seen as ending at 16 or 18, and until school buildings become community education centres, then this continuity will not occur. One thing is certain: if practical ability is not used continuously, then individuals will lose the priceless facility they have developed during their time at school. Almost everyone knows individuals who personally regret this loss.

REFERENCES

Burnett, M. (Ed.), *Music Education Review*, Vol. I, Chappell, 1977.
Burnett, M. and Lawrence, I., *Music Education Review*, Vol. II, NFER-Nelson, 1979.
Carlton, M., 'Wind Band Repertory', *Music in Education*, March, 1978.
Central Advisory Council for Education, *Half Our Future*, the Newsom Report, HMSO, 1963.
East, J. M, 'The School Orchestra: Building a Programme', *Music in Education*, November, 1978.
Light, P., 'Starting and Developing a Wind Band', *Music in Education*, March, 1978.
Schaeffer, D., *Take It!* (an introduction to improvisation for jazz ensemble), Pro Art, 1975.

REPERTOIRE/RESOURCES

Advice on repertoire for the various ensembles may usually be gained from instrumental teachers, and many local authorities maintain central libraries of sets of music from which schools and colleges are able to borrow.

To supplement this it is worth noting that publishers' catalogues offer graded series, for example the *Chester String Orchestra* or *Just Brass* series or those from Chappell, Belwin Mills or Hal Leonard.

Additionally the two volumes of *Music Education Review* noted above provide details of 'recently' published music for ensembles.

There is a good deal of knowledge and experience available for teachers to draw upon (except possibly in the fields of ethnic music) and therefore a short list of available books follows:

Alford, C., *An Introduction to the Sitar*, Keith Prowse, 1973.
Avtarvir, R., *Learn to Play the Sitar*, Pankaj, New Delhi, 1980.
Bartholomew, J., *The Steel Band*, O.U.P., 1980.
Minority Group Support Service, *The Sound of Steel*, Coventry Education Authority.
Noel, T., *The Steel Band*, Commonwealth Institute.
Sealey, J. and Malm, K., *Music in the Caribbean*, Hodder & Stoughton, 1982.

CHAPTER TWELVE

Instrumental Teaching
in Schools

... for parents and teachers

The first known instrumental teaching in schools can be traced back to the late nineteenth century at Uppingham and Harrow, both public schools, whereas in state schools it is a relatively recent innovation. In the 1940s, following the end of the second world war, education authorities in some areas, notably the London County Council, instituted an instrumental teaching service, a practice since adopted by all authorities in England. Now, in many cases, after less than thirty years, as a result of economic and political pressures, a number have either discontinued the service or introduced a financial contribution from the parents towards the cost of each lesson. Although other aspects of the state system are free to all pupils, the pressure is such that the only way to ensure that instrumental teaching survives is to impose a levy on those benefiting from the service. Not all authorities have succumbed, particularly those in some of the larger cities where it is evident that the introduction of charges would see the disappearance of instrumental teaching overnight. The implications of all this, specifically in inner-city areas, are undesirable especially in times of high unemployment where the imposition of further financial strain on the poorer families merely assures as always that the pupils will be the losers. Whatever moral stance is taken over the whole business of making selective charges within a state system of education, it must be accepted that there is little, if any, logic in penalizing those pupils who have obvious musical ability.

Why should all this pressure be directed against instrumental teaching? There are number of possible reasons, but primarily this aspect of education is seen by many as being peripheral, largely because of the way the instrumental teaching service has developed, been organized and taught. Traditionally instrumental lessons, especially those for piano, were provided from the private sector; it was never until recently thought to be a responsibility of the education authorities to provide these facilities.

Generally the pattern of development has been for instrumental teachers – sometimes referred to as peripatetics – to be under the control of the music adviser for each authority, and their teaching programme to be controlled solely by her. The teachers' base has tended to be at a music centre or sometimes the office of the music adviser, but rarely a school. The adviser would attempt to share out the teaching time as fairly as possible between a number of schools. Such a system inevitably developed faults simply because in the process of trying to share out insufficient teachers, the tendency is to teach for shorter periods of time in a considerable number of schools rather than for large blocks of time in a few centres. Shorter periods mean more travelling time between schools and consequently in the end less teaching. Until recently instrumental teaching took place during school hours, but coupled with the introduction of charges, the pattern is now varied to include evening teaching within schools and music centres.

So, one way or another, the instrumental teacher is seen either as a person who merely visits a school for a limited period of time each week, or as someone who teaches in a music centre and never actually enters the school. Whichever policy is adopted there is little opportunity for the instrumental teacher to contribute consciously to the whole curriculum, to know well the pupils being taught or how the instruction given relates to overall development, all quite indefensible postures in any cost-effective or educationally viable analyses. So an unfortunate sequence of developments in times of economic strength has led towards undermining the present instrumental teaching service.

An experienced teacher who has worked both as an instrumental and classroom pedagogue recently wrote:

On the whole, instrumental teaching must be getting worse. Fifteen years ago all instrumental teaching was done by 'sessional' people who were in the main, professional players. Professional players can no longer do the work because many are not qualified to teach. It is now done by people who do not truly know whether they are teachers or players. When you think of it, how many young professional players do you hear of who were initially taught by a peripatetic teacher? They all seem to have had private lessons from a professional. Presumably peripatetic instrumental teaching will continue in its present, barely acceptable form, until such time as one visionary music adviser stops building his empire for a few years in order to devote himself to improving the total system, for the benefit of all.

The case has no doubt been overstated and thankfully the system is not designed solely to produce professional players but nevertheless it is worth considering what aspects of the service are likely to change in the future.

There are conflicting views about the role of instrumental teachers, but the weight of opinion seems to be directed towards training them to fulfil a much broader function, including teaching in the classroom. A growing number of new entrants into the profession have expressed a wish to combine both class and instrumental teaching, and using this ability for example in urban areas, they could be attached to a group of schools such as one secondary and its feeder primary schools. Each teacher would be officially on the staff of one of the schools and be involved in the life of the school as fully as possible within the time available; they would teach say at least half a day in the classroom if the opportunity arose.

The group of schools would co-operate to organize the instrumental teaching; numbers and timetables would need careful consideration, but there are obvious advantages in such a scheme. The teachers themselves would have a sense of purpose, direction and a feeling of belonging to a particular school in which they have a firmly established base. Wasteful travelling would be cut to the minimum if schools were in close vicinity to each other. The instrumental teacher together with the class teacher could become fully involved in the follow-up work and would be able to organize combined instrumental ensembles from all the schools and thereby ensure continuity of teaching from primary to secondary school. Much follow-up work takes place extra-timetable and although class teachers willingly work the extended day without additional payment, as the system is organized at present many instrumental teachers are rarely involved to any extent.

It should be mentioned that few groups of schools would be likely to require the full-time services of say either a bassoon or oboe teacher and these would therefore adopt a peripatetic role in the original sense of the word.

SELECTING PUPILS

There are often more pupils wanting to learn than there are instruments available, and so it may be necessary for the teacher to implement a selection process. A common method used is to discover whether a pupil can sing in tune, hear and repeat short melodic phrases and hear and clap easy rhythm patterns. Alternatively standard tests such as those of Wing and Bentley may be used. Testing of musical aptitude is an unreliable process as many instrumental teachers will confirm; pupils who have responded well to tests do not always reveal the musical aptitude expected at a later stage of development. There is of course no way of knowing whether the tests have excluded pupils with latent talent or those who respond badly to any form of testing.

The Wing *Standardized Tests of Musical Intelligence* (1968), or Wing battery as they are sometimes known, are designed to be administered as a group test; they are recorded and only piano sounds are used. In the first test the pupil has to decide how many notes are played in a chord, and in the second to indicate whether any note has changed when the chord is played for the second time. The third is a tonal memory exercise where a melodic phrase is played twice and the pupil has to identify which note has changed in the second playing. The tests become progressively more difficult, but beyond those described, are rarely used for initial selection purposes.

Arnold Bentley's *Musical Ability in Children and its Measurement* (1966) is again intended for group use but it is recommended that young children of seven and under should be tested individually. In contrast to Wing, the Bentley tests use pipe organ and pure electronic sounds for the exercise. The four areas of testing are sense of pitch, tonal memory, chord analysis and rhythmic memory. The first uses twenty pairs of *sine tones** for pitch discrimination and the second consists of ten five-note melodies played on the organ with each note being of equal duration. For the third, the pupil has to decide how many notes are played in a chord, while in the last area comparison of rhythms is demanded.

Some other tests available are listed at the end of this chapter. The fallibility of the tests persuades many teachers to allow as many pupils

---

*a 'pure' electronically produced tone (without the addition of harmonics)

as possible to begin playing an instrument and after a period of time make an assessment of the pupil's likely ability, interest and staying power, bearing in mind the overall educational justification for the service in the first place.

FOR PARENTS – SELECTION OF TEACHERS

If instrumental lessons are provided by the school, the parent has little or no choice in selecting a teacher, but if it is decided to pay for private lessons outside the school, there are points to bear in mind. The world of music enables teachers to take examinations, usually diplomas which if successful allow the person to use 'letters' after the name, for example, ARCM (Associate of the Royal College of Music), or LRAM (Licentiate of the Royal Academy of Music). There are many such qualifications; the majority, such as those described, are perfectly acceptable, but parents should be aware of some which are bogus. Advice on this point may always be sought from the school music specialist if there is any doubt. Qualifications on paper are important but there are other considerations, for example, the question of finding a teacher who is compatible with the pupil and who can provide a happy but stimulating situation in which the pupil may thrive.

A child of eight from a musical family began to take violin lessons at school from the visiting instrumental teacher and at the same time piano lessons from a private teacher. The boy enjoyed playing the violin, despite the fact that in his particular school music was viewed as an extra. The instrumental teacher, sensitive to this problem, felt it was essential to show positive results to prove the value of the work. The result for this particular boy was a lessening of interest, because the lesson became an occasion for weekly testing rather than one of providing an enjoyable and possibly more productive experience.

The boy continued to have piano lessons although rejecting daily practice sessions. However, interest was maintained and some progress made, because the teacher was able to motivate the child sufficiently from week to week without the external pressure the violin teacher had to overcome. The pupil surmounted various technical obstacles without realizing it; to admonish for not practising would in this case have merely deterred progress and possibly destroyed interest completely. The teacher never lost sight of how playing the piano had to fit into the boy's lifestyle, and showed a remarkable ability to guide the pupil through a maze of problems to a stage from which more advanced development could emerge.

It is a question of being able to find a teacher who treats each pupil as an individual, a teacher who is not a slave to the examination system and a teacher who is prepared to see the role the lessons have to play in each pupil's life.

GROUP OR INDIVIDUAL TEACHING?

Within the state system it is likely that the initial learning experience will take place within a group varying from four to 12 in number, but many authorities make provision for individual tuition at a more advanced stage. At the beginner level, a teacher may cope adequately with three or four pupils every half-hour, but as ability develops in pupils, it becomes an impossibility to hear prepared work, look critically at it and organize tasks for the week ahead under these conditions. Certainly at the early stage of learning an instrument there is no evidence to suggest that pupils necessarily benefit from individual tuition, but what is apparent is the skill required by the instrumental teacher to design a programme of learning for each individual within a group situation. The ability to ensure progress, interest and involvement for all pupils is one which requires considerable experience to develop, but those who have coped in the classroom with thirty pupils, where the same requirements are demanded, often find it easier to apply the principles to instrumental teaching. The advantages of group teaching are obvious:

1. they are cost-effective;
2. the support of the group can be very important to each pupil during the early learning stages;
3. the group provides opportunity for ensemble work from the outset within the lesson time.

There are few publications to help teachers with group work, but useful reference books particularly for string teachers are those by Sheila Nelson published by Boosey and Hawkes, and similar publications from the Belwin Mills catalogue.

Although it is generally accepted that individual tuition becomes necessary at a later stage, this position has never been authoritatively researched. Master classes work effectively in groups and there is no reason why, with skilled teaching, this could not be applied to almost all instrumental tuition. It is an area which deserves further consideration, especially if it is accepted that instrumental teaching is not only about producing technicians, but developing technique through interpretation and involvement.

ESSENTIAL SUPPORT FOR THE PUPIL

No matter how highly motivated a pupil might be, she will need support beyond that which can be given by the instrumental teacher. She will require support in the form of encouragement and practice facilities at home; at school certainly encouragement, possibly practice facilities where these are not readily available at home, and the opportunity to make full use of practical ability by taking part in ensemble work.

Many pupils do not sustain instrumental lessons for the duration of their school life. Most teachers have formulated views as to why this is, but again unfortunately there is little factual information available about this under-researched problem. If any of the support aspects already discussed are not forthcoming, the pupil may quickly be discouraged sufficiently to give up the work. A positive way of ensuring this does not occur is to set up lines of communication between school, parent and instrumental teacher and to actively encourage parents to be involved in or observe the early stages of learning.

It is most important that instrumental teachers attend school open evenings when parents discuss general progress with subject or class teachers; it would be a small step towards establishing that instrumental teaching makes a positive contribution to the curriculum for some pupils.

The relationship between the teacher and pupil may be a contributory factor to the rate of drop-out. In what may be a one-to-one relationship, some compatibility is essential, compatibility not only in personality but also in aims. The question of encouragement has already been mentioned; beyond this pupils need to be presented with material to play which maintains their interest and which continues to present a challenge. Inflexible programmes offered to all pupils are positively harmful, that is to say working slavishly and systematically through a 'method' book. For example, many young violinists long to use the bow almost as soon as they pick up the instrument for the first time, and yet are prevented from doing so by a teacher who insists on a certain stage of development being reached before this is permitted. Such a restrictive attitude can lead to a lessening of motivation on the part of the pupil; enthusiasm often runs high in the early stages of learning an instrument, and the teacher has to build on this so that it becomes strong enough to carry the pupil through the difficult period which is likely to follow.

A further reason for discouragement may arise from the experience of playing an instrument which may be quite acceptable but only at a very elementary stage. Non-musicians find it difficult to understand how important it is to feel comfortable with an instrument and particularly with the sound it can produce. Professionals frequently change instruments in a search for the ideal partner in the playing process; the same situation exists if to a lesser degree with children. Recently a pupil was learning to play the trumpet but was becoming progressively more frustrated at the inability to produce an acceptable sound. After some delay this particular pupil was loaned a different trumpet on the recommendation of the instrumental teacher; the difference in the pupil's playing was quite remarkable, and previous insuperable problems vanished almost without trace. This pupil was on the point of giving up instrumental work until the change of instrument was made; the first instrument was not a particularly bad one, it simply did not suit the individual.

Conflict of interests may add to the various reasons for giving up lessons. The adolescent world is full of other attractions which are infinitely more acceptable than that of practising alone in a room. The instrumentalist is an 'oddity' in society, and it requires a strong and determined character to pursue such an interest when other friends are involved in leisure activities whether sporting, going to discos or simply enjoying the company of their peers. Within the school, the musician may find similar conflict if he is also gifted in other areas which do not always demand the essential personal discipline required when learning an instrument; it can be a very lonely pursuit. The conflict may be greatest if individual instrumental progress is slow, for example, it can be very difficult for the string player trying desperately hard to cope with elementary pieces when she lives in a society where many talented musicians contribute so much to the adolescent world. She must almost inevitably compare her ability with that which is presented through the commercial recording world.

Follow-up work by the school may be as important as providing the actual lessons for the pupils. Playing together in bands and orchestras can have a stimulating effect on players and particularly so for the beginner. These activities unquestionably contribute to maintaining interest and promoting development.

The chapter on the primary school (Chapter 4, p. 41) should also be referred to in matters concerning choice of instruments. More particularly both parents and teachers should refer to the often neglected but vital consideration of dental care for wind players (Chapter 4, p. 38).

CONCLUSION

The fundamental question, 'What is the purpose of the instrumental teaching service?' will always be at the forefront of the minds of music teachers. Whether it be to provide for the very talented (as discussed in the next chapter) or to ensure that opportunities exist for all as with other areas of the curriculum, will continue to be a matter for debate.

If it is accepted that extra-timetable activities should be viewed as an intrinsic part of the educational programme of a school, then the same must be said about instrumental tuition. Suitable provision for the gifted generally in education has in recent years been officially recognized; the pupils with musical ability cannot be excluded from this policy.

REFERENCES

Bentley, A., *Musical Ability in Children and its Measurement*, Harrap, 1966.
Brace, G., *Music in the Secondary School Timetable*, University of Exeter, 1970.
Wing, *Standardized Tests of Musical Intelligence*, O.U.P., 1948.

SUGGESTED FURTHER READING

Collins, S., 'Peripatetic Music', *Times Educational Supplement*, 4 Feb. 1977.
Farmer, P., 'A State of Inequality', *Times Educational Supplement*, 4 Feb. 1977.
Porter, M. M., *The Embouchure*, Boosey & Hawkes, 1967.
Porter, M. M., 'Dental Problems in Wind Instrument Playing', *British Dental Journal*, 17 Oct., 7, 14 and 21 Nov., 5, 12 and 19 Dec. 1967.
Oxford University Press, *Instrumental Technique Series* (which includes lists of pieces for each instrument).
Rees, W. I., 'Why Do Children Drop Instrumental Tuition?' *Music in Education*, January, 1978.

ACHIEVEMENT AND ABILITY TESTING

Colwell, R., *Music Achievement Tests*, Follett Educational Corporation, Chicago, 1968–
    70.
Colwell, R., *The Evaluation of Music Teaching and Learning*, Prentice-Hall, 1970.
Gordon, M., *Musical Aptitude Profile*, Houghton Mifflin, 1965.
Lehman, P.R., *Tests and Measurements in Music*, Foundation of Music Education
    Series, Prentice-Hall, 1968.
Seashore, C., Lewis, D., and Saetveit, J., *Seashore: Measures of Musical Talent*, The
    Psychological Corporation, New York, 1960.

CHAPTER THIRTEEN

Musically Gifted Pupils

... of particular concern to parents

Parents are more likely than teachers to be concerned about the musically gifted. Their child has begun to have piano lessons and has made exceptional progress, or even without lessons has begun to pick out tunes on an instrument. Is he or she musically gifted and what should the parents do about it? Alternatively after a period of time, their son or daughter has shown remarkable progress and ability on an instrument; what action should parents take to ensure that the development continues?

As a parent it is difficult to be objective about one's own children and take an unemotional and analytical view of the child's real ability and potential; it is necessary to be guided by musicians or music teachers but, as with medical conditions, a second opinion may be valuable.

A parent may seek help from any of the following:

    a. the pupil's instrumental teacher
    b. the school music specialist
    c. a local prominent musician
    d. the local authority music adviser or
    e. at the appropriate age for entry, the head of a special school as identified later in this chapter.

This chapter will provide sufficient background and information to help when such an approach is made, and provide a basis for discussion. It may help parents initially to decide whether the child really is gifted or talented and whether they ought to ensure that special help is forthcoming, or indeed whether to pursue a special type of education within one of the few schools available.

General Ability

Establishing a definition of giftedness is not easy; the simplest but in many ways the least satisfactory is to say that a gifted child is very intelligent and this intelligence may be measured by the many tests available. It is usually accepted that children with an IQ of around 140, or slightly lower, fall into the category of gifted children in terms of general ability. De Haan and Havighurst in *Educating Gifted Children* (1961), state that intellectual ability is composed of various parts referred to as 'primary mental abilities' which constitute 'areas of talent'. They are: verbal skill, spatial imagination, science, mechanism, art, music and social leadership. Accordingly, it is argued, the gifted child may be defined as an individual who is 'in the top 10% of his age-group in one or more of the areas listed'. The view is also canvassed that no child ought to be designated as gifted without displaying the ability to produce imaginative and original work. No account of creativity is measured in intelligence tests which are largely concerned with assessing mechanical intellectual qualities and it would be necessary to support these with an overall view of the pupil's work over a period of time.

The Schools Council project *Gifted Children in Primary Schools* (1973) formulated the following definition as a basis for enquiry:

The term 'gifted' is used to indicate any child who is outstanding in either a general or specific ability, in a relatively broad or narrow field of endeavour ... Where generally recognized tests exist as say in the case of 'intelligence' then 'giftedness' would be defined by test scores. Where no recognized tests exist it can be assumed that the subjective opinions of 'experts' in various fields on the creative qualities of originality and imagination displayed would be the criteria we have in mind.

Musical Giftedness

Using the previous statement as a guideline makes defining musical giftedness no easier task. Many people feel confident that they can identify a musically gifted person, but it is more than likely that they have in mind the image of a fluent, polished performer possessing outstanding qualities which are universally recognized, a person in the category of genius or prodigy such as a Menuhin.

The problem is how to define exactly what musical giftedness is and to establish whether other individuals with lesser ability than the exceptionally gifted can be placed within the definition. Where is the dividing line between giftedness and non-giftedness? There is an awareness that we are surrounded by able musicians and although none may approach the category of a Menuhin, all, as a result of their abilities, have considerable influence on the lives of people with whom they come into contact. Is this a factor to be considered?

Musicians themselves perceive giftedness in a very narrow way and tend to relate it to the individual who succeeds as a performer on the concert platform, a view undoubtedly formulated as a direct result of their own particular musical education. Is musical giftedness related only to performing ability and can it be measured purely as technical skill? How does the composer fit into the definition? There are many known examples of talented writers whose ability is not matched by their practical skill as a performer.

In the eyes of many musicians and teachers the whole of the pop world is seen as a grey area containing few able musicians, and yet nothing could be further from the truth; in particular, groups and bands have to write and perform their own material if they are to develop any individual identity. Are such people to be seriously considered?

Similarly in the small and big-band world of the semi-professional musician there are many extremely able, talented and creative individuals who, because of the nature of the work, are unable to make a living purely by playing; nevertheless for those people music is the main interest in their lives. Are these also to be considered?

The church organist may devote her life and abilities, however limited, to promoting music within the church and the immediate community; many survive a routine job of work to earn sufficient money to allow themselves to become fully involved in the music of the church, which is their main interest.

For similar reasons, the school music teacher may have an even wider influence on the community and on the lives of young people; in this case giftedness may need to be defined much more broadly. Is such a person, who probably possesses a wide range of ability without necessarily excelling in any particular one, to be considered?

Towards a Definition

An appraisal of the individuals I recall and consider to be musically gifted reveals two factors. First, that I find it impossible to define clearly why I consider each individual to be musically gifted, but that I have reached the conclusions purely on the basis of my own experience as a musician. Second, all those I consider to be gifted are totally involved in music to the extent that it has become the source of motivation for the individual and a prime reason for living. Additionally all have achieved a fair degree of proficiency on a musical instrument to the extent of allowing them to interpret and communicate freely through performance. Sheer technical skill is not sufficient on its own; all have developed the ability to communicate at their level of skill.

We do, although perhaps undesirably so, see musicians in some sort of rank order; musicians frequently refer to others as being for example, either 'exceptionally gifted' or at the other extreme 'not very gifted', but again these tend to be very much individual assessments. It is noticeable though that when placed in the position of assessing others, a panel of experienced musicians rarely finds it difficult to agree in broad terms as to a person's ability, although it may be more of a problem to define clearly why a particular view has been formed.

Giftedness in music may cover a much wider range of ability than is generally accepted; it cannot only be applied to pure skill and technique, but must include other allied and indefinable qualities which are common to the arts and are not to be measured by testing, for example creative and imaginative qualities. How or whether the giftedness develops may be a matter of chance, but we can only attempt to measure that which has developed. Such development depends on opportunity, support and encouragement, the right teacher or the availability of resources such as instruments at the appropriate time. In retrospect many adults are able to relate to an actual time when it became apparent that music was going to play an important role in their lives and yet, for some, the opportunity to develop interest and ability may never occur.

In the Calouste Gulbenkian Foundation Report *The Arts in Schools* (1982), a definition is established which takes the view that the *gifted* are those with exceptional flair for 'expression and communication through the arts'. They are those who are at the summit of their profession as composers or performers.

The report states that the *talented* are those possessing outstanding ability but to a lesser degree than the gifted and obviously these will be greater in number. The dividing line is blurred simply because at the early stages potential is all that is being considered and much will depend on the opportunities provided as to how this will develop.

Recognition of Musically Gifted Children

Some work has been produced on recognition although it is somewhat limited; the whole area is under-researched. It is mentioned in the Schools Council *Gifted Children in Primary Schools* (1973), in the form of an extract from *Mens en Musick* (1958) which refers to distinguishing marks of the musical prodigy:

1. Abnormally keen ear.
2. Phenomenal musical memory.
3. The child listens for a considerable period to a particular instrument and then expresses a strong desire to play it.
4. The child plays fluently and even performs in public with distinction before he has learnt to read the notation.
5. A high degree of talent for an instrument is sometimes shown by facility in playing without looking for the notes.
6. The child prefers his chosen instrument to any other plaything or occupation.
7. He becomes completely absorbed in making music, so that his instrument seems an inseparable part of his personality.
8. He is self-possessed in performance and does not suffer from stage fright.
9. He improvises spontaneously.
10. Genius is shown not merely through technical mastery, but through the creative ability with which the child interprets the music.

The Schools Council enquiry asked teachers what forms of behavioural evidence they would expect to find in musically gifted children. These characteristics were, in their opinion:

1. A sense of rhythm.
2. Rapid learning of an instrument.
3. Aesthetic appreciation of tonal quality.
4. Ability to sing in tune.
5. Sense of 'pitch' and harmony; aural perception of a high standard.
6. A musical memory.
7. Imaginative tune-making.
8. Rapid adaptability to new rhythms.
9. Spontaneous improvisation.
10. Feeling for melody and phrasing.

Music educationists would challenge lists such as these, primarily because the criteria lack definition and are by inference linked to a music education which has strong connections with the music of the 18th and 19th centuries: for example, the reference to 'feeling for melody and phrasing' and 'imaginative tune-making' may have little bearing for any child who has developed through an education programme which is based largely on the music of this century. It suggests other questions which would need to be answered, for example 'What is a tune?', 'What is a good tune?', 'What is an imaginative tune?', 'Is a tune the appropriate form for the child to make?'. Much contemporary music is concerned with texture rather than melody and harmony.

The exceptionally gifted child may be easy to recognize providing that there is ample opportunity for her to reveal her ability within the music activities of the school. There are pupils however, who, because of pressure from parents and teachers to be involved in all things musical both at home and at school, resist the unbearable demands made on their ability, and consequently restrict musical activity to the home and community outside the school. To recognize such a situation, the music teacher has to be alert and hope that through contact with parents and previous schools the problem can be handled sympathetically.

The view is generally held that an exceptionally gifted child will, no matter what obstacles are placed in the way, find a path through the system. This may possibly be true, but it must be realized that the problems faced by children and parents in coping with exceptional ability can be enormous.

In secondary schools where music is not accepted on a par with other subjects, the musically gifted child may be forced to pursue her interest and ability entirely within the surroundings of the home in order not to be seen as the odd one out in the school situation. Such a child may therefore never be recognized at school or provided for accordingly within the curriculum. Some children are able to modify their outward and visible reactions, thus allowing themselves to be accepted as full members of the various social groups in the school while pursuing their particular interest in a self-contained way; they develop a personality which fulfils this dual role.

Teachers and parents are often too concerned about being unable to recognize ability and seek a series of criteria on which to base any judgement, but it is worth remembering that there are many known cases of talented musicians, acknowledged to be gifted performers, who simply cannot successfully complete tests which measure potential musical aptitude (such as those described in Chapter 12, p. 122).

Provision for the Musically Gifted

Whether the musically gifted should be educated in a 'normal' school or have the opportunity of attending a special music school is a continuing matter of debate. The arguments in favour of the normal school include the view that gifted pupils have a better chance of developing emotionally and socially, and that to separate them from their peers would merely be to compound the problems associated with being gifted.

Against this opinion is the feeling that few schools have the staffing or flexibility of timetable to allow for giftedness to develop. From early teens most pupils are working towards public examinations and, no matter the degree of giftedness, too often there is an insistence that music must play a subordinate role to other areas of the curriculum.

Extra provision to compensate may of course be provided by the local education authority.

At the other end of the ability spectrum, as a result of the Warnock Report, *Special Educational Needs: Report of the Committee of Inquiry into the Education of Handicapped Children and Young Persons* (1978), there is now pressure to bring certain categories of mentally and physically handicapped pupils out of special schools and into normal schools. It is unlikely, therefore, that in the future the state system will provide special schools for the gifted if there is a move towards bringing others into the normal system. Even where there is considerable ability, it has to be acknowledged that without an education which spans a broad curriculum, gifted musicians may be restricted to a career only within the music industry.

Existing Special Music Schools

The arguments in favour of special schools are counter to the ones already expressed; here the pupils follow a curriculum built around their giftedness. They have the advantage of working in a school conducive to their interests and also of sharing experiences with their musical peers. A pupil following his special interest, which is seen as such and supported by the school, is relieved of musical frustration.

Progress is rapid and this rubs off onto other areas of work, disproving the belief that general education may suffer.

As will now be seen, provision for a music-based education lies mostly outside the state system.

Chetham's School in Manchester has always had a strong musical tradition, but not until 1969 did it become a specialist music school. The only entry qualification is that pupils must be 'gifted' in music. Most of the 300 pupils are between the ages of 11 and 18, and although in the private sector, a large proportion are supported financially by their own local education authorities.

Wells Cathedral School, Wells, Somerset, is an ancient choir school founded in the 12th century, and has over 600 pupils between the ages of seven and 18. Of these about 70 undertake specialist musical training coupled with their general education; 16 of these are also cathedral choristers. A further substantial number of pupils have instrumental lessons but have no special ability or pretension towards a career in music.

The Purcell School, Harrow, previously the Central Tutorial School for Young Musicians, was renamed in 1973. The school caters for between 100 and 150 pupils from the ages of 8 to 18; it accepts those possessing exceptional musical ability and others with some expertise who wish to benefit from a music-oriented education.

Yehudi Menuhin School, Stoke D'Abernon, Surrey. This small select school of some 40 pupils founded in 1963 is for those between the ages of 8 and 18; it concentrates solely on pupils with outstanding ability.

Pimlico School, London. This unique school within the state system has a small intake of musically able pupils in each year of the school, despite the obvious conflict with the comprehensive ideal. The pupils are selected from the whole of the Inner London Education Authority area after being assessed in aural perception, improvising ability and general commitment.

Military Academies. In an unpublished thesis, 'The Special Needs and Problems of the Musically Gifted' (1979), Victor Payne describes the visits he also made to military training establishments, which are in a rather different category from schools. He says: 'the ultimate view of the value of potential is reflected by the military establishments that train musicians where it is stated, "It is not necessary for a junior to play an instrument before enlisting. If he is keen to learn and has the aptitude, he can be trained".'.

The military academies take teenage boys who often have little in terms of educational qualifications and in some cases no musical accomplishment. They then provide a suitable environment for growth, an environment which has produced many gifted musicians – it is simply a way of developing talent that is different from that of the school.

Victor Payne goes on to summarize:

Although marked differences of attitude and style could be observed in each of the special schools, variations of practice regarding educative and musical processes were less apparent. To some extent at least, the term *junior academies* could be applied to all if this is taken to imply a junior version of traditional conservatoire practice in this country. As may be observed at the senior level, different attitudes to, for instance, new music and the broader reaches of musical talent, exist seemingly as degrees of tolerance rather than as positive and integral forces. It is true that some of the special schools appear to have adopted a more child-centred view than others but, in musical and general educational terms, there was little evidence of any radical development. ... The opportunities that exist in such schools as these for education *through* music as well as education *in* music appear to be as yet virtually untapped.

CONCLUSION

It is regrettable that the state education system has failed to make adequate provision for the exceptionally gifted child in music. On the surface it may appear that the instrumental teaching service is providing this in the form of individual lessons and group experience. Those involved in music education know only too well that the development of instrumental technique and skill is only part of the essential provision if the end product is to be a thinking, feeling musician rather than a musical automaton.

The growth of the instrumental teaching service together with new attitudes towards curriculum planning have allowed many pupils to fulfil potential which otherwise would have remained undiscovered, but here too, in general, the emphasis has been on the development of instrumental skill. An exceptional pupil will need to follow an individual curriculum which places greater emphasis on music than is usual, together with provision for practice within school time where facilities are available. It is nonsense to suggest that a pupil should wait until homework is complete at the end of the day before he can make use of his most obvious talent. Similarly provision must be made for talented pupils to fully develop their creative abilities in what is both a performing and creative art.

Here then is an area of music education into which more research will hopefully be forthcoming. Until such time, it is worth reflecting on the value of the exercise of defining giftedness when we are neither providing the situations in which such talent may develop, nor acknowledging those who would benefit from the provisions described.

REFERENCES

De Haan, R. F., and Havighurst, R. J., *Educating Gifted Children*, University of Chicago Press, 1961.

Gulbenkian Report, *Training Musicians*, Gulbenkian Foundation, 1978.

The Arts in School, Gulbenkian Foundation, 1982.

Ogilvie, E., *Gifted Children in Primary Schools*, Schools Council Research Studies, 1973.

Payne, V. W., 'The Special Needs and Problems of the Musically Gifted', unpublished M.Phil. thesis, University of York, 1979.

Warnock Report, *Special Educational Needs: Report of the Committee of Inquiry into the Education of Handicapped Children and Young Persons*, HMSO, 1978.

SUGGESTED FURTHER READING

Burt, C., *The Gifted Child*, Hodder & Stoughton, 1975.

Department of Education and Science, *Gifted Children in Middle and Comprehensive Schools*, HMSO, London, 1977.

Fenby, E., *Menuhin's House of Music*, Icon Books, 1969.

Freeman, J., *Clever Children, A Parent's Guide*, Hamlyn Press, 1982.

Gibson, J., and Chennells, P., *Gifted Children. Looking to the Future*, Latimer with the National Association for Gifted Children, London, 1976.

Jewell, D., 'The Lonely Making of a Modern Virtuoso' (a profile of Mike Oldfield), *Sunday Times*, 5 Dec. 1978.

Musical Giftedness in the Primary School, UK Council for music education and training, Pullen, 1982.

Payne, V. W., 'A Suitable Soil for Growth', *Times Educational Supplement*, 24 Oct. 1975.

Pickard, P. M., *If You Think Your Child is Gifted*, George Allen & Unwin, 1976.

Povey, R., *Educating the Gifted Child*, Harper & Row, 1979.

Small, C., 'Music School at Ormskirk', *Music in Education*, Vol. 38, No. 367, May/June 1974.

CHAPTER FOURTEEN

Conclusion

It can be seen that within the last thirty years a number of important changes have taken place in music in education, not least the realization (especially in secondary education) that the music curriculum has a role to play in the educative process of all pupils, and not only for the talented minority. Music specialists in secondary schools are usually overburdened teachers attempting to foster and monitor a wide range of activities which take place outside the normal timetable; nevertheless they have shown a growing awareness that it is the classroom music which directly affects all pupils. In the past (largely as a result of teachers' personal enthusiasms being reflected in extra-timetable activities) this was a neglected area; the balance is being redressed.

Teachers have been compelled to re-examine curriculum aims and content particularly in the light of research produced during the 1960s showing total rejection of classroom music by many pupils. Curriculum, especially in the secondary field, has broadened from being a purely re-creative subject to include creative activity, now acknowledged under the umbrella title of composition. Generally speaking instrumental work in the classroom is more in evidence than vocal activity, but this could be viewed as part of the process of providing content acceptable to pupils; technological developments have made this an even more attractive proposition now that synthesisers, computers and basic recording equipment are available within the financial budget of many schools.

The new thinking and changing attitudes on the part of teachers are beginning to ensure that the curriculum reflects the music not only of the pupils' world but of society in general. Pop and rock music contribute towards the curriculum as does contemporary 'serious' music, both of which readily reveal themselves in the compositional work undertaken by pupils.

The influence of Orff, Self, Paynter and Murray Schafer in effecting curriculum change culminated in the Schools Council project *Music in the Secondary School Curriculum.* On the other hand primary schools, which led the way in the 1950s and '60s with imaginative use of voices and instruments, were served by an earlier Schools Council project which was seen by many to be a retrograde document, largely because of emphasis placed on the development of musical literacy. Yet the report was an attempt to provide teachers with a programmed approach in order to ensure that a music curriculum was implemented despite the lack of co-ordinating specialists in these schools.

One of the major benefits for pupils during the last thirty years has been the growth of the instrumental teaching service, which at its zenith fulfilled the educationally desirable notion of providing tuition for almost all interested pupils. It is a particular area of education which has reflected the economic prosperity of the country and in consequence is now, to a certain extent, in a state of decline. The service has enjoyed spectacular success resulting in large numbers of pupils playing in ensembles of various kinds, and continues to be of obvious benefit not only to individual pupils, but to the school community in general.

The growth of the instrumental teaching service has helped to reveal a number of obviously gifted pupils. Giftedness in music is an area into which more research is required, but some progress has been made in identifying the qualities of such pupils. The number of schools available to provide a specialized education for the gifted is limited and lies largely outside the state system; not all teachers, however, are convinced that these pupils are better provided for in a school which concentrates on the giftedness at the expense of a broader general education.

Whether evaluating musical programmes for the gifted or for others, music teachers have only recently attempted to come to terms with the growing demand for accountability. No longer is it acceptable to say that the arts are incapable of being evaluated and assessed. As far as music is concerned, assessing practical performance poses few difficulties; but assessing composition is problematical largely because it is an activity outside the personal experience of many teachers. Much more research has still to be carried out into evaluation and assessment of the music curriculum, but some help is given to teachers in Chapter 10.

Finally it is worth noting that music plays an important part in the lives of most people in the western world, although the involvement may be of a passive nature. There is likely to be an increase in leisure time generally in the future and in consequence people will search for activities to fill the vacuum created by shorter working hours or unemployment. Many will turn to music in some form or other. It will be important therefore for schools to ensure that future citizens are equipped with musical skills and experience on which to build in later life.

Index